SHRAPNEL

By the same author

Birdy
Dad
A Midnight Clear
Scumbler
Pride
Tidings
Franky Furbo
Last Lovers
Wrongful Deaths (memoir)
Houseboat on the Seine (memoir)

WILLIAM WHARTON

Shrapnel

The Friday Project
An imprint of HarperCollins*Publishers*
77–85 Fulham Palace Road
Hammersmith, London W6 8JB

www.harpercollins.co.uk

First published in Great Britain by The Friday Project in 2012
Copyright © William Wharton 2012

1

William Wharton asserts the moral right to
be identified as the author of this work

A catalogue record for this book
is available from the British Library

978-0-00-745807-3

Typeset by Palimpsest Book Production Limited
Falkirk, Stirlingshire
Printed and bound in Great Britain by
Clays Ltd, St Ives plc

PROLOGUE

When we had little children, four of them, they always wanted me to tell them stories and I enjoyed the telling, but there were certain tales I never told. I'd developed the storytelling habit as a young boy, less than ten, making up scary stories for my younger sister.

Most of the tales I told to our children were about a fox named Franky Furbo. I told these stories from 1956, when our oldest daughter was four, until 1978 when our youngest was twelve. Mostly I told 'get up' stories in the morning while they were fresh and so was I, not bedtime stories.

We were lucky because, through most of my adult life, I did not leave home to work a job, and often, our children did not go to school. In a certain way, these stories were part of their schooling. Franky Furbo, among others, was a good teacher.

But sometimes our children wanted stories not about Franky Furbo but about other things, such as my childhood experiences, or fairy tales which ended with 'and they lived happily ever after'. Our oldest daughter called these Ever After stories. Or occasionally, they wanted what they called 'war stories', tales about what happened to me during the course of World War II.

I generally didn't want to tell those tales and tried to divert them, but children can be awfully persistent, so when I did tell tales about the war, they would be relatively amusing incidents, different ways of foraging for food, or evading various regulations, unimportant events of that nature.

In my book *Birdy*, in the penultimate chapter, I develop an important war experience, one of the types of tales I didn't tell our children. The entire book *A Midnight Clear* revolves around another tale. I wrote *A Midnight Clear* because I thought we were about to re-establish the draft of young men, to send them off to kill or to be killed. I felt an obligation to tell something about war as I knew it, in all its absurdity.

One evening in New York I had dinner with Kurt Vonnegut. He asked me, 'How was your war?' I flippantly responded by recounting the number of court martials in which I'd been involved. It was not a good answer. War for me, though brief, had been a soul-shaking trauma. I was scared, miserable, and I lost confidence in human beings, especially myself. It was a very unhappy experience.

It was not a pleasant experience writing this book either. When dug up, the buried guilts of youth smell of dirty rags and old blood. There are many things that happened to me, and because of me, of which I am not proud, events impossible to defend now; callousness, cowardice, cupidity, deception. I did not tell these stories to my children. My ego wasn't strong enough to handle it then, perhaps it isn't even now, when I'm over seventy years old. We shall see.

I did write out many of these unacceptable experiences just after I came home when the war was over. I was fifty per cent disabled, and a newly enrolled student at UCLA. I cried too easily, made few friends, and couldn't sleep. I'd stay up nights when I couldn't sleep, trying to write the events, my feelings, my sense of loss, ineptitude. I had changed from an engineering major to an art major. I took a job as night watchman in a small notions store. I wanted to be a painter, but in the back of that store where I was night watchman, I was learning to be a writer and didn't know it. Each dawn I'd read over what I'd written, tear it into pieces, and flush it.

There is written into *Birdy* one of the first really negative experiences I had in the military. It involved shovelling coal outside Harrisburg on a cold December morning. I hit a man with a shovel and was threatened with a summary court martial. Actually it was so summary, my only punishment was that I was confined to quarters until they shipped me out for infantry basic at Fort Benning, Georgia. It was the first in a series of my personal reactions to the constrictions and expectations of the military.

The conditioning of soldiers, so they will respond to command without question, was an abomination to me. Also, the rigid hierarchy on vested authority was an insult to my personal sense of identity, of value. I fought the military mentality with my meagre resources but to no avail. In the end they prevailed. They taught me to kill. They trained me to abandon my natural desire to live, survive, and to risk my life for reasons I often did not understand and sometimes did not accept.

1. BASIC TRAINING

I. BASIC TRAINING

BIRNBAUM

Basic training in Fort Benning, Georgia, in 1944 was a minimum of twelve weeks. During this time we suffered through thirty mile long hikes, rifle range, infiltration courses, crawling under machine guns firing over us, all the nonsense and misery the army can think up.

There is a young man in our outfit called Birnbaum (his name means 'a pear tree'.) He is Jewish and really wants to learn how to be a soldier so he can kill Germans. He's more aware of the horror and racism of Hitler's world than most of us.

Birnbaum is a great clod, a real *klutz*, a *zaftig*, a baby-faced fellow with two left hands and two left feet. It seems he can never do anything right, buttoning his clothes is a challenge for him. Even with help, he can barely make his bunk up to pass inspection. He isn't a goof-off on purpose; he's really trying to do what's asked of him. It is absolutely pitiful. His inept concentration on the simplest of tasks could bring tears to your eyes. He just does things wrong somehow, no matter how much we all try to help him.

At each Saturday inspection, poor Birnbaum has something wrong, his webbing will be dirty or tangled, his entrenching tool dirty, his canteen or mess cup filthy, coated with sugar, stained brown by coffee, or something critical is missing from his full field pack. The military punishes not just the individual. Birnbaum is given additional KP or some messy job such as cleaning the latrines, and they cancel weekend passes into town for the whole squad or platoon.

On one general field inspection, our entire company has its weekend leave revoked. So, it isn't out of pure altruism that we all try to help Birnbaum – we're going stir crazy. The non-coms and officers in charge just can't seem to accept the obvious fact that Birnbaum is never going to be their kind of soldier. We do everything we can, but the more we try, the worse he gets.

For daily rifle inspection, we have an absolutely vicious Lieutenant. He's part of the regular training group, called the *cadre*, pronounced not as one syllable as in the original French. Lieutenant Perkins is from Tennessee, a former member of the Tennessee National Guard, and he really takes it out on poor Birnbaum.

Once, we do get Birnbaum through barracks inspection. We've already missed two weekend passes in a row so we all pitch in. We scrub his webbing clean, polish his shoes, make him practise his manual of arms until he's perfect, at least as perfect at that kind of dumb thing as Birnbaum is ever going to be. All that's left is rifle inspection out on the drill field.

My job is to make sure his rifle's clean. I break it down completely. I run rifle patch after rifle patch through the barrel until I've shined even the worst of the pits. I scrape out the ridge in the butt plate, oil the strap, even polish the firing pin. As a finale, I steal some steel wool from the mess hall kitchen. It's strictly forbidden to pull steel wool through an M1 rifle bore but I've found this to be a sure way to get that ultimate sheen when an inspecting non-com, using his thumbnail as a mirror, peers down the rifle barrel. He wants to see the pink of his nail reflected along its full length with only the thin, graceful line of rifling showing.

So now we're ready for the ultimate test. We closely examine Birnbaum for unbuttoned buttons, and set his field cap so it's exactly straight, two fingers width above his right eyebrow as the army insists. We give him a brief review on how not to get his butt plate dirty when he's at order arms or at ease. We review how he's to let go of his rifle as fast as possible on 'present arms'. We're sure Perkins will pick on Birnbaum, he always does.

One of the crazy things about military inspection is the ritual of checking to see if our rifles are clean. We'll all be standing in a line with our rifles at our sides. An officer will yell 'attention', then, 'present arms', followed by, 'inspection arms'. We all, in a prescribed manner, hold our rifles out in front of us and snap the bolt open with our thumbs. The inspection officer then strides casually in front of us, looking us over, looking for something wrong, a cap askew, a button unbuttoned, a speck of dirt, etc. Then, at whim, he'll stop in front of one soldier and stare at him. He can do anything, ask questions, comment on an article of clothing or a haircut, whatever.

Usually a non-com goes along behind taking notes on what the officer says and putting a soldier on report. Not good. When the officer in charge stops in front of you, he's most likely going to inspect your rifle. That is, he's going to snap that rifle out of your hands. If he does it correctly, from his point of view, wrong from yours, the butt will swing in and crack you in the groin. Our aim is to practise so we can let go of the rifle as fast as possible, ideally, so fast he'll miss it, drop it.

We're watching his eyes and shoulder for signals. He's trying to fake us out. If we drop the rifle and he doesn't swing out for it, we're dead. We really only hope to let go in time so we won't be hurt. However, in the back of our evil hearts we pray for that miracle of miracles when he'll swing, miss, and drop the rifle. We've heard of it happening but have never seen it. The regimental rule is that if an officer drops a rifle it's his responsibility to clean it to the soldier's satisfaction.

Well, Birnbaum is never going to reach the point where an officer would drop a rifle. We work hard just to help him avoid instant emasculation. This I've seen often enough, the unfortunate soldier grovelling in the dirt, hands gripping groin, trying not to scream. Twice this has already happened to Birnbaum, once he vomited over Lieutenant Perkins' shoes. But this time he lets go of it fine. A wave of pleasure can be felt along the entire squad. Perkins inspects the butt plate, the swivels, the action, and then he inserts his thumbnail in the bolt for barrel inspection. I'm feeling confident – I'd inspected that barrel just before putting it in the barracks' rifle rack, before lights out. It was perfect.

Lieutenant Perkins continues to stare down the barrel. He shifts to get better light on his thumbnail, he peers with his other eye. His face goes white. Then red. I'm two soldiers to the right, and wondering what can be wrong. Lieutenant Perkins looks down at the ground then up at the sky. He hands the rifle to Corporal Muller, just behind him. Muller sticks his nail bitten thumb in and almost gets his eyeball stuck in the end of the rifle barrel he stares so long and hard. Muller's hands start to shake. He looks over at Perkins, then down the barrel one more time. His jaw is stuck between hanging open and clamping shut in fury. He faces Birnbaum.

'Private Birnbaum, what the hell have you done to this rifle?'

'I cleaned it, Sir.'

Birnbaum squares his sloped shoulders. One should never call a non-com Sir, that's reserved for officers, but at this moment this indiscretion is being ignored.

Muller takes a deep breath and then looks down the barrel again. Lt Perkins takes it from Muller, stares down the barrel as if to verify his worst fears.

'Soldier, what the hell did you use to clean this rifle anyway, sulphuric acid?'

'Steel wool, steel wool, Sir, steel wool!'

The whole rank can hear Birnbaum, I feel sweat trickling down my back. Lt Perkins turns to Muller.

'Put this man on report, Corporal.'

He turns to Birnbaum.

'Soldier, you're confined to quarters until I can get together a court martial.'

For once our passes aren't cancelled, but poor Birnbaum is left alone in the barracks.

Before I leave for town, I ask him what the devil happened, I can't understand. It turns out, Birnbaum, in his eagerness, in his anxiety, his desire to please, had stayed awake all night, in the dark, running steel wool up and down inside that barrel.

Later, I get to peer down that now infamous rifle and it isn't like a rifle at all. Birnbaum has been so industrious he's worn out all the rifling and virtually converted it to a twelve or fourteen gauge shotgun. It's clean all right; however, any ordinary thirty-calibre bullet would probably just fall or wobble out the end of that rifle when fired.

There's a summary court martial, Birnbaum must pay eighty-seven dollars to replace the rifle. All his gear is removed from our barracks and he's sent elsewhere. None of us ever sees him again. 'Steel wool!' becomes the rallying call of our squad.

I hope Birnbaum survived the war. He'd probably have made a good soldier. If there is such a thing.

WILLIAMS

A friend named Williams had been in charge of
training Birnbaum for the daily rifle drill. After
the court martial, he determines to exact revenge
for Birnbaum by faking Perkins into dropping his
rifle. The idea has a certain appeal, and so he
manages to involve me. We stand by the hour,
facing each other, practising, taking turns playing
officer, feinting, trying to fake each other into
making a false move. We both become better as
officers than as enlisted men being inspected. But
we also become fearsomely quick at letting the
rifle drop. It comes to the point where we can
read any slight signal of eye or body, I'll swear
Williams can even read my mind. Whenever either
of us can get the 'officer' to miss, drop the rifle,
he wins a quarter. After two weeks, I'm almost

three dollars in debt. That's a huge sum when your salary is fifty-four dollars a month.

Finally, basic training is behind us and we're approaching final inspection, after which we'll be shipped out. We'll be going out to other infantry divisions being formed, or directly overseas as replacements. It's beginning to look as if all the rifle snatching practice is going to naught, and Williams is fit to be tied.

For some reason, since Birnbaum, no officer or non-com has stopped at either of us and gone for our rifles. But then, on the big day, full dress parade, it happens. Only it doesn't happen the way it should. Lieutenant Perkins, with a Captain beside him stops at *me*. I should have known, they'd never stop at Williams. He's so spic and span, real soldierly looking, they'd never bother. I'd never be his kind of perfect.

I don't even have time to think – after so much practice it's automatic. At a slight wince in Perkins' eye I let go of that rifle. The rifle spins and hits the dirt, the front sight gashing Perkins' finger on the way down. I know Williams must be excited, happy. At the same time, disappointed because they'd passed him by. I'm just scared. I stare ahead with my hands still in the present arms position, looking straight where I'm supposed to be looking, not down at the rifle. Perkins looks briefly at his gashed finger then holds it out from his side so no blood will drip on his suntans. He glares into my eyes.

'At ease, soldier.'

I take the position the military calls 'at ease'. That is, you spread your legs about eighteen inches apart, stiff-legged. If I'd had my rifle, I'd have gone into something called 'parade rest'.

'Soldier, deliver that rifle to the orderly room when inspection is over.'

'Yes, Sir.'

He wheels away, still holding his hand out at his side. The Captain takes over the rest of the inspection. I know I'm on 'private report' and dread what is sure to come.

The rifle is still lying in the parade ground dust and dirt. I reach down and pick it up. I'm probably breaking at least five army rules doing this, but I don't care. I love that rifle. I've carefully zeroed it in to 'expert' level for everything from two hundred to five hundred yards. I still remember the serial number of that rifle, 880144.

The crazy thing, among many crazy things, is when I finally do go overseas, they issue me a *new* rifle, one I didn't get to zero in, don't know at all. I feel nothing for that rifle. I kill human beings with that 'piece' but it's never really mine. I feel I don't actually do it. Maybe that's the way military planners want it to be – nothing personal.

When we get back to the barracks, Williams is frantic with excitement. He pulls me aside and into the latrine. He has a paper sack full of coal dust and a tube of airplane glue. I watch, numb, as he mixes them into a gooey running paste and pours this mess down my rifle barrel and into the action. He's trembling with a combination of fury and mirth.

'Now that bastard's really got something to work with. Birnbaum's revenge. I'm almost tempted to include a package of steel wool.'

I decide that would be too much, they might stand me up before a firing squad.

I deliver the rifle, with Williams pushing behind me, to the orderly room. We dash back to the barracks. Next morning the rifle is delivered by the mail clerk, it's like new. I check the serial number and it's mine all right. I don't know who cleaned out that mess, or how. Not a word is said. I hope it's Muller, I'm sure it isn't Perkins – I suspect it's the mail clerk.

We ship out three days later. I'm sent to Fort
Jackson, South Carolina, to an infantry division.
I'm hoping I'll never see Lieutenant Perkins again
and I don't look very hard.

CORBEIL

During basic I got to know Corbeil, the fellow who sleeps in the bunk below me. He's one of the few in our group who has much education beyond high school. He'd been in the Master's programme at Columbia when they drafted him and he hates the army even more than I do. He'd been a philosophy major with a special interest in existentialism, and considers the whole war an uncalled for, unjustified, interruption of his life. His name is Max and he reads books, half of them are in French, which he had sent from home. He considers the post library a literary garbage pit. I'll admit I don't even know where the post library *is*. One weekend he comes back from town with an alarm clock. Now the last thing in the world you need in the army is an alarm clock.

Regularly, before light, about fivethirty, the Corporal of the Guard comes through yelling. He makes sure everyone's rolled out of bed, he's kicking the beds as he goes along, yelling and hollering. If you pull your covers over your head he'll rip them off the bed and dump them on the floor. This means starting the bed from scratch.

Most of us make the bed for Saturday inspection, and then slip ourselves under those blankets like letters into envelopes the rest of the week. We slide out the same way. These blankets are virtually glued to the frames. That way we can snatch a few minutes in the latrine before the thundering herd descends upon us.

By six we need to be lined up in the company street, dressed, shaved, clean, with our rifles and helmet liners. There'll be roll call, the orders of the day, a few kindly words from Muller or Perkins about what rotten soldiers we are, then we go to mess hall for breakfast. The KP have already been rousted out at four.

I ask Corbeil, incredulously, 'Why the alarm clock?'

Corbeil holds the clock next to his ear and smiles. 'This little ticker's going to get me out of the army.'

I figure all the reading has pushed him over the

edge. My mother always insisted reading softens the brain.

That night I hear him wind his clock. I hang over the edge of my bunk and watch as he tucks it under his pillow. In the dark of night I hear it go off. I'm a relatively light sleeper. He lies still for a few minutes, then carefully slides out of his bed onto his knees. He pulls his top blanket off the bed onto the floor. Then, still kneeling, he starts peeing on the bed, spraying back and forth. Using a penlight, he resets his clock, pulls his still dry pillow off the bed and wraps himself in the blanket on the floor.

I again hear the alarm go off just before the Corporal of the Guard comes at five thirty. He jumps up, hides his clock on one of the rafters to the barracks, then curls up in his blanket again.

After roll call, he takes all his wet bedding to the supply sergeant and gets new ones. This happens every morning for a week. Muller becomes a raving maniac. He puts Corbeil on sick call. They give him some pills he doesn't take. He offers them to me. After a week, the supply sergeant won't give him any more clean bedding and they take his stinking mattress away.

Corbeil starts sleeping with just a blanket over

the metal slats of his bunk. But the alarm keeps going off and, in the dark, I can hear the splash as he pees on his sheet. It begins to get awfully smelly around our bunk.

As far as I know, besides Corbeil, I'm the only one who knows what's happening. After two weeks they send Corbeil to a doctor, then a psychiatrist. When he's around with the rest of us, not on sick call or in the hospital, he does his work like everybody else.

Muller is all over Corbeil, calls him 'piss head' and even more vulgar names. Corbeil is very modest, sorry about everything. He even gets a bucket of hot soapy water and scrubs the saturated floorboards under his bed. He apologises to everybody, claims this had been a problem for him all his life. Far as I know, he didn't have any trouble until he bought that damned alarm clock.

One day he doesn't come back from sick call. He's gone for almost a week. I borrow a few books from his footlocker. Even with the ones in English, I can't understand them.

I begin to sleep through the night and things smell better under the bunks.

He comes back smiling. They've issued him a mattress, mattress cover, blankets. That night I hear the alarm go off again. I listen as he goes through his full routine. I need to hold my mouth to keep from laughing, and the whole double bunk shakes. Corbeil looks over the edge of my bunk.

'Take it easy, Wharton, it won't be long now. Wait till tomorrow.'

He resets his alarm and goes to sleep. Corporal Muller screams, hollers and curses Corbeil. Non-coms aren't allowed to touch enlisted men, but he comes close, nose to nose, spittle flying. This is an insult to the whole US Army, he claims. He rants and raves, makes Corbeil wash the blankets, the mattress cover, air out the mattress.

But nothing is going to stop Corbeil. He's removed from the barracks again. The alarm clock is still in its hiding place. I wait. About three days later, we come in from field exercises and there's Corbeil. He's emptying his footlocker into his duffel bag. He's wearing his dress uniform, not fatigues. He smiles at me. I wait until nobody is close by. Everybody's in the latrine washing up. We'd just spent the day in a dusty field learning the difference between creep and crawl. You creep like a baby and crawl like a snake. I think, or it could be the other way round.

I put my rifle in the rack. I'm covered with mud, a combination of dust and sweat.

'So, what happened.'

'I did it. I'm out. I've got a medical discharge, honourable. In three days I'll be home. I'll just have enough time to enrol in school on a late registration. I've got "enuresis". The US Army can't use me. Isn't that too bad?'

He smiles and jumps up to where he keeps his clock. 'Here, take this. It's a gift for keeping quiet and not giving me away. I'm sorry to have wakened you, and for the stink, but I don't want to be dead. Bodies smell worse.'

So, he gets out of the army. In a few days we have a replacement from another company named Gettinger. Gettinger goes down with us to Fort Jackson, South Carolina, and we go through a lot together. He's killed outside Metz. One thing I learn is it pays to have a university education.

LOGAN

About two weeks after the alarm clock business, we're hanging around the bulletin board outside the orderly room. I'm with a fellow named Logan. He's from Steubenville, Ohio, and is the only one of us who receives money from home in addition to his monthly pay.

Logan receives one hundred and fifty dollars monthly. Logan has good reason to hate the army.

He'd been an air cadet. He'd become battalion commander of his cadet class. They were preparing for graduation, after which they would all become Second Lieutenants. Logan was drilling his battalion in close order drill, marching, high stepping smartly, backward down the company street when he was hit by a jeep from the rear. He spent three weeks in the hospital with broken ribs and a cracked collarbone. When he came out, he was classified as unfit to be an air cadet and was transferred to the infantry.

He still, illegally, has a complete Second Lieutenant's uniform, tailor made, down to the gold bars. He'd had them ordered before he was clobbered. Officers, because they are officially gentlemen, need to buy their own uniforms. Even now, as an enlisted man, he still has his shirts and fatigues tailored. He has them dry cleaned and pressed, off post. Except for the missing bars he looks more like an officer than most of our real, so called, officers and gentlemen.

One day there's an announcement on the bulletin board telling about two openings as 'cook's helpers' and asking for volunteers. 'Cook's helper' is the army's way of saying KP pusher. We've just had a miserable day in the field making a march wearing gas masks, through waves of tear gas. Anything looks better.

Logan stuffs the notice in his tailored pocket. We go up the steps to the orderly room and officially volunteer our services to Reilly, the company clerk. He tells us we're the first to volunteer; we know we'll be the last. The next day, at roll call, we're told to report to the orderly room.

Lieutenant Gross, the executive officer, tells us

we are taken off the regular roster and temporarily reassigned to Sergeant Mooney, the cook, as helpers. We are to report right away to the kitchen and Sergeant Mooney. We salute our way out and start to worry. It all seems too easy – generally, volunteering in the army is a dumb idea.

But it turns out to be *really* great. Mooney is fat and sloppy. He likes to eat and likes to drink, but he doesn't like to cook. Whenever I read the comic, *Beetle Bailey*, I think of Sergeant Mooney.

Our job is to wake the KPs at four am, get them down to the kitchen, assign duties, and have things ready for breakfast at seven. Theoretically, we aren't supposed to do anything ourselves, just make sure the KPs get the work done. We stay on at night until the kitchen is clean and the dining hall ready for the next day's breakfast.

The thing that makes it great is we're on a day, and off a day, taking turns. If the company clerk and executive officer agree, we can even have passes to town on our days off. Also, even when we're on duty, there'll always be a few hours after lunch and before dinner when we can take turns going back to the barracks and resting. We're living in luxury. That alarm clock Corbeil gave me in basic comes in handy.

Now, in general, KP pushers are loved just about

as much in the army as trusties are in jail. They're considered finks. They've sold their souls to the devil. Logan and I decide to change this around. One of the prime power plays of KP pushers is the assignment of jobs. Those go all the way from the easiest, that is serving and setting tables, to the worst, 'pots and pans'. We immediately let it be known that it will be first-come, first-serve from now on. Whoever gets there first gets the first choice of jobs. I even rent out my alarm clock a few times when I'm not on duty.

Then we begin getting more and more done in the evening before we shut down the kitchen, so we can wake the KPs later in the morning. We have a good breakfast made for the KPs with eggs, scrambled or fried, four or five strips of bacon, orange juice, cereal, milk and coffee. Nobody else is eating like the KPs except us. It turns out that Logan, besides liking fine clothes, likes good food and can cook, a real Epicurean.

As long as things get done in the kitchen, the cook couldn't care less. He never comes in till O six hundred anyway. We begin waking KPs at O five hundred instead of O four hundred. Because neither of us is a particularly aggressive or hostile type, we gradually bring the KPs onto our side, or, maybe, we go over to the side of the KPs, whichever way you want to look at it. We're friends to everybody.

The cook is satisfied because we're getting the work done, so he has hardly anything to do. We develop all kinds of short cuts, more efficient ways to do things, not a particularly difficult task.

Logan and I work out a system to keep the stove burning overnight by feeding it just before lights-out and wrapping the coal in wet newspapers. So now the KPs come into a nice warm kitchen, with the tables set and most of the work already done. We begin to think being cooks would be great. The cook even recommends that we be sent to cook's school. Also, our company is the only one where everybody is begging to be on KP. Logan figures if we can gain control of the KP lists, we can even *charge!*

We gradually find out that the food being served is so terrible because of the way it's cooked. Nobody in the country is eating the way we're supposed to be being fed. It's actually food fit for kings. These great big beautiful pork chops come in, at a time when meat rationing is tough for civilians, and this cook takes those hundreds of pork chops and dumps them in a big pot of boiling water. Then he pulls them out dripping wet and gives them a little frying on the griddle with greasy oil so they'll look better, as if they'd been fried or roasted. But they taste like cardboard and are as tough as shoe leather. They only look like pork chops. We talk the cook into letting us do more and more of the cooking while he sinks slowly into his private stew, alcohol.

Logan is teaching me how to cook. We start making things like Beef Stroganoff instead of stew, chipped beef in garlic sauce instead of 'shit on a shingle'. We even get so we can do a fair job of broiling steaks, giving a choice: rare, medium or well done. That's quite a trick with two hundred people to be fed in less than an hour. The KPs get into the spirit. The Captain promotes the cook from staff to tech.

Around this time, some of us are given a chance to take our first furlough. I go home to California where my folks have moved from Philadelphia while I've been gone. Logan will take his furlough when I come back. He'll double up and handle both ends of the job, do all the cooking. I have twelve days travel time. This plus the ten-day furlough comes to twenty-two days. With a little manoeuvring on the weekends at each end, I have twenty-four days altogether. I feel paroled. I'm going to be out of the army, on my own, after almost six months as a prisoner. It seems like a dream come true.

For the first time I visit my parents in California. I meet the woman who becomes my wife six years later. We dance a lot. There are great bands, big swing bands in Southern California then. We dance at the Casa Manana and the Casino Ballroom. Jimmy Dorsey, Harry James, all the big ones play. Most of the men dancing are in uniform. It's a great furlough. When I come back, I find I've been put onto the duty roster again! I can't believe it.

Logan is at cook's school and the cook had been broken to private. There's another cook who doesn't want cook's helpers, KP pushers. I'm back on the line in a line outfit. I feel I've been rooked. I have been!

Much later, I learn that in the battle of the Ardennes when everybody, truck drivers, clerks, cooks, even the regimental band are put up on the line, Logan shoots himself in the arm with a carbine. If you do a thing like that you're supposed to hold your hand over the rifle and shoot through a cloth, between the bones. I thought he'd have done a better job of it. Or maybe it really *was* an accident.

2. FORT JACKSON, SOUTH CAROLINA

SERGEANT HUNT

Before we're shipped overseas, I've been reassigned to Regimental Intelligence and Reconnaissance, called I&R. Somebody scanned my records and found my AGCT score. I move from K Company to Regimental Headquarters company.

It's even better than being a KP pusher. We're given special training in patrolling, using high tech (for the army that is) phones and radios, we get to drive jeeps, trucks and weasels. Weasels are a kind of personnel carrier that has tracks and can go through water. We're even sent back to Benning for parachute jump training. In two weeks we make five jumps. They won't let us make the sixth because then we'd be eligible for paratrooper jumping wings, which would have given us fifteen dollars extra a month.

The Master Sergeant of Regimental Headquarters is a special kind of person. He could well be one of the meanest people I will ever know, but he is always smiling and laughing. He has small eyes and a big stomach. He's 'regular army' and a southerner. I don't know how smart he actually is, but when it comes to running an infantry company he's a genius. He runs a company as if it's his own private army, set up for his personal profit. We privates, and everyone else, are his serfs.

The Company Commander and other officers love him because they don't have to do anything. The Company Commander is just decoration in this company. Twice Sergeant Hunt is offered a commission and refuses. He lives better, eats better, and makes more money with all his schemes, than the Regimental Commander.

But he makes one mistake. He gets too greedy; and somebody, somewhere along the line, discovers that Hunt's been having marital allotment cheques sent to three different women in three different states. He's a trigamist. He could get away with this because he signs the allotments himself. He has one wife in Alabama, one in South Carolina and another in Mississippi. There's a court martial and he's broken all the way down to Private. He has to make up for the fraudulent allotments and he does. I think he's a rich man by that time, anyway.

Anyone else would have wound up in Leavenworth, but he can call in some of his chits, and officers like him. He's moved into the regular barracks like the rest of us, and we have a new Master Sergeant shipped in.

Now everyone who'd ever been given a hard time by him jumps on *Private* Hunt. His life isn't worth living. Shaving cream is squeezed into his toothpaste tube, he's short-sheeted every night and has to remake his bed before he climbs into it. There can be anything, spiders, scorpions, snakes, condoms full of water, anything, under those blankets. But he never says anything, he just smiles, crinkling his eyes; throws these things on the floor, and puts everything back together.

He has all the shit details; latrine duty, KP, and pulls hard guard. Even lousy PFCs try to make his life miserable. He only smiles his fat smile with flesh bunched up around those small eyes. To me he looks more dangerous this way, his shirt sleeves showing where his old master stripes had been when he was top kick. I make a point of staying away from him.

He's older than any of the company officers, including the new CO, by far. Probably in his late thirties, he seems like an old man to us. He just keeps his mouth shut, does whatever he's told, no matter what, even things he doesn't have to do, like mop the barracks floor every morning before reveille. And nobody knows arm regulations, word and verse, as Hunt does. I'm convinced something bad is coming.

It doesn't take long. He somehow manages to be transferred to 'C' Company. Then, nobody ever went up through the ranks the way Hunt does. He stitches each new rank on with big loose stitches until he's finally back to three up, three down, with the diamond of a Master Sergeant. These he stitches on tightly.

Starting right then, he begins arranging transfers from Headquarters to C Company of about twenty non-coms and PFCs. These twenty are those who had given him the worst time. We all go down to look at the bulletin board every morning with dread. We never hear from any of those soldiers again except to see their names on the demotions list, if they had any rank. He wears them down, one at a time. Since then, I've harboured a fear of big, smiling, fat, southerners. It's a form of personal bigotry.

WATER

At Fort Jackson, the last part of our training is a series of thirty-mile 'water hikes'. We hike thirty miles in one day, camp overnight, then come back thirty miles the next. We do this on one canteen of water, so we go sixty miles on a quart of water, which isn't much, because it's hot and humid.

Right away, a friend of mine, named Pete, decides he's going into business. He solders, or tapes together, three number ten cans with the bottoms and tops cut off of them; I don't know how he does it, but he does. He even builds in a small plug. I watch him do this after field duties, in the dark, and I begin to think he's going crazy.

We normally carry a full field pack on those hikes, along with our M1s, ammo and bandoleers. The rest of the pack is our mess kit, blankets wrapped around a tent, a tent pole, tent pegs and underwear. We carry it vertically sticking up higher than our heads, and it weighs about sixty pounds with everything in it.

Now Pete has several gallons of water in his contraption, but no shelter half, no blankets, no tent pole, no tent pegs. I know a cubic foot of water weighs about seventy pounds, so it's heavy. When we go out on the hike, he straps his water on his back. I admit, it looks like a regular field pack.

At the end of the hike, at the bivouac, everyone is dying of thirst. It's very difficult not to drink water on the way, and there's no water out there. The officers make the trip in jeeps, blowing dust in our faces as they go by with Jerry cans full of water. The idea is for us to fill up with as much water as we can before we start, then keep our water drinking down. But everyone is perspiring and urinating, so we're lucky if we can save half a canteen for the night and the next day.

My mouth starts sticking to itself, my tongue to the top of my mouth, my teeth to my lips, my lips to each other. After a few hours our tongues are hanging out of our mouths.

Pete starts charging two dollars for a canteen cup half full of water. He must have twenty canteens full in that pack, which is a lot of money. But he winds up with no shelter half, no blankets, no tent pole, no tent pegs. He has no place to sleep.

Luckily for him, it's a hot night and he camps out behind my tent. We pile a bunch of brush and pine needles around him so nobody will see him.

Now, the way you build a tent in the army is this. Each GI carries a half tent called a shelter half. Then two GIs get together, button the shelter halves together, and using two tent poles and all the tent pegs, have enough for a tent. Pete's tent buddy, who isn't in on the water ploy at all, has half a tent. All he can do is hide, along with Pete, trying to sleep under his shelter half. He definitely isn't happy about this whole shenanigan.

But Pete pulls this nutty thing off. He divvies the water out until he has over forty dollars. He gives five of this to his deprived tent mate to shut him up. But he makes one mistake, he forgets to save any water for himself. However, this looks good in terms of his alibi if he needs one. He's as thirsty, or thirstier, than any of us. He's almost outfoxed himself. The good thing is that his full field pack is empty and doesn't weigh more than ten pounds on the way back. But Pete's problem is he likes to gamble. Within a week, he loses his thirty-five dollars, plus a bit more.

Of course, something like this can't be kept quiet; the whole squad thinks it's so incredible. The platoon leader finds out and calls Pete in. He asks if he's really done it. Pete denies everything and insists somebody made it up. He shows he has no money, and by this time, he's gotten rid of the cans. There's no evidence whatsoever.

I'm sure the officers think it's a pretty good scam, too, because no one ever does persecute or prosecute Pete, or even try to make his life miserable. But they check everybody's full field pack after that. From then on, our 'water marches' are for real.

3. SHIPPING OUT

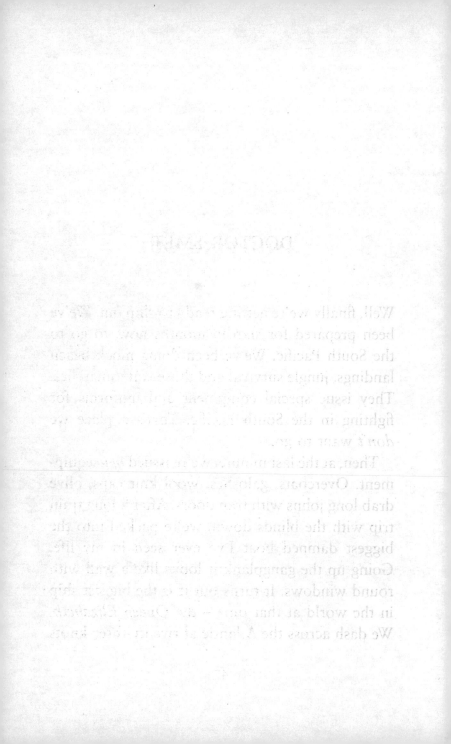

DOCTOR SMET

Well, finally we're getting ready to ship out. We've been prepared for sixteen months now, to go to the South Pacific. We've been doing mock beach landings, jungle survival and those water marches. They issue special equipment and uniforms for fighting in the South Pacific. That's a place we *don't* want to go.

Then, at the last minute, we're issued *new* equipment. Overcoats, galoshes, wool knit caps, olive drab long johns with trap doors. After a long train trip with the blinds down, we're packed into the biggest damned boat I've ever seen in my life. Going up the gangplank it looks like a wall with round windows. It turns out it *is* the biggest ship in the world at that time – the *Queen Elizabeth*. We dash across the Atlantic at twenty-three knots per hour in five days, without escort. We're supposed to be faster than submarines can shoot or something like that. But I doubt it, I rarely take my life jacket off. There are fifteen thousand of us packed into that ship, most of us are seasick after the first day. I spend as much time as possible floating in an old bathtub I find. The water sloshes over the sides with each lurch, but I stay more or less steady, waterlogged but not sick. Simple physics.

Eight of us pack a tiny third class cabin built for two. The mess lines are so long, one can just finish one meal in time to stand in line for the next, but most of us aren't into eating much anyway.

We land in Scotland, and are then shunted from train to train. European trains, all darkened, shades drawn, with little cabins, chock full, smothering in full field packs and new uniforms. Finally, in the middle of the night, we arrive at what had been an old textile mill in the town. We're supposed to be hidden here, for who knows how long. But this is impossible. You can't really hide a whole division and there's division after division hidden all over England waiting for the big moment.

We're virtual prisoners in that smelly mill. Then

somebody finds out that a black transportation unit had stayed in this mill just before us. So, without asking anybody, the goofy southern crackers throw all the mattresses out the window, into the courtyard, and burn them. After that, we sleep on the woven canvas straps of the bunks. Max Corbeil would have felt right at home.

One day I'm picked for a detail moving officers' footlockers out of some trucks. I don't know what these officers store in these footlockers, but they're heavy enough for dead bodies. There are too many officers and not enough enlisted men in a Regimental Headquarters Company.

Pushing a heavy one up onto a truck, I really hurt myself. I'm sure I have a hernia, I *hope* I have a hernia. I'm transported to a hospital in a civilian ambulance. It turns out what I've done is develop a varicocele. I don't know what it is, but hope it's serious. It turns out to be a varicose vein in one of my testicles. It's tender and I can feel it, like little worms, but it's not what the doctors call 'disabling'. We're within weeks of the big move, nobody knows anything for sure, and if they do, they're not telling.

I spend as much time as possible complaining, writhing, moaning, groaning. They give me a little canvas bag to wear on my balls. It's like a cross between a G-string and a jock strap. They even give me an extra for when one gets too smelly. Two days later a doctor stands at the foot of my bed. He smiles.

'I guess we ought to operate on this, but it's not going to kill you and you won't need to do any heavy lifting.'

I can tell he's never carried a full field pack or an officer's footlocker.

'You just stay in bed here and I'll have you back to your outfit in no time. Don't you worry about it.'

He says this as if 'getting back to my outfit' is my fondest dream, like going home.

After he leaves, I'm really in pain; mental anguish. This could have been the chance of a lifetime for me to stay in England, practically like a civilian for the whole damned war.

My prime qualification is as rifleman. That's the worst MOS you can have. The second worst is scout, that's *my* second MOS, but my third is typist. I'd learned to type in high school and had gotten a good score on the army typing test. It's my ace in the hole, a deep hole, unfortunately probably a foxhole. I know that if the outfit leaves without me, they'd need me in England. I'll volunteer to type out forms, or maybe some Major's personal war novel. Anything. My fingers itch to type.

The next time Doctor Smet comes around I'm curled up in agony out of habit more than anything; but he's written off that varicocele. Yes sir, he's going to do me a big favour and get me back to my outfit. He's my friend. He's going to save me from that nasty operation. I think he expects me to kiss his hand.

But now, of all things, he becomes interested in my right foot. I've always had a bump sticking out on the back of my right heel, since I was a kid. Whenever I buy new shoes I develop a blister there. It's one of those things you learn to live with. He probes it with a finger, then a needle. He tries jiggling it back and forth. He keeps asking me if it hurts and I yowl. Tears come to my eyes. He writes on his little clipboard.

He brings another doctor over to look at it. I scream some more, pretending to be brave. He tells me I have what's called a calcaneus spur. He asks me if it hurts when I walk.

'Well, yes Sir, it does. It gets all red and swells up on marches and I have blisters it's so sore.'

He writes some more on his clipboard. Maybe I have a second shot at England.

I'm in the hospital four more days. Every time

I have a chance, and nobody's looking, I bang that calcaneus spur on the metal siding of the bed. I start limping when I go to the bathroom. It begins to hurt so much I need to limp. I stay awake and moan at night a lot. The nurses give me aspirins to shut me up.

The next day, Doctor Smet comes around with another doctor. This one seems to be a specialist. He turns me on my stomach, bends my knee up, twists my ankle in all directions and starts hitting the back of my foot with a little rubber hammer.

Of course, I'm screaming, howling, the whole time. I don't need to fake it much because with all my thumping on the bed, that foot's practically a piece of hamburger meat. The two doctors step back from the bed, 'consultation time' I figure. Maybe they'll decide to discharge me, give me a medical discharge. I'll have a disability pension. The second doctor comes up to the side of the bed. He has his clipboard at his side.

'You're in Headquarters Company, Regimental Headquarters, isn't that right Soldier?'

'Yes sir, I&R.'

'Well, you won't need to march much then. Just take care of that foot.' He writes on the clipboard. He looks down at me and winks.

Doctors, especially military doctors, should *never* wink.

'I'm assigning you back to duty. The nurse will give you some Band-Aids for that foot. Nice try.'

And so the future painter, engineer, teacher, psychologist, writer is condemned to death, with a wink!

NEED A BODY CRY

When I come back to our mattress-less mill, I flop out on the canvas strap bed, trying to get it into my mind that I'm still in the army, the same army. All I have to show for my medical malingering is two dinky 'ball holders' and a sore Band-Aided foot. It isn't an hour later when Diffendorf, our balding mail orderly, comes in. He's the one who first announced to me the happy fact that I would be balder than he is before I reach thirty. Perhaps it was a classic example of a self-fulfilling prophecy. Anyway, from then on, I'm aware of my constantly expanding forehead. I now have a forehead that goes practically all the way down the back of my neck, a fore and aft affair.

This time Diffendorf gleefully announces to me

that the regimental S2, Major Love, wants to see me, and on the double.

I change shirts, check buttons, brush the fronts of my new combat boots on the back of my pants. This is just dumb habit. The boots are clean, and the shiny leather is inside, the outside is rough like suede, 'All the better to absorb water with, my dear.' Blotter boots.

I hustle up the street of this small English town called Biddulph in the middle of the Midlands of nowhere. The S2 has his headquarters in the city hall. It's one of the few buildings in town that still has the ornamental iron fence in front of it. All other gates, fences, grilles have been ripped out and contributed to the war effort, melted down and turned into shrapnel, I suppose. I dash past the sentry at the ornamental gate. His name is Thompson, he plays trumpet in the regimental band. As I dash by, he tries to hide a cigarette.

Inside, Taylor, Love's assistant, is sitting at a desk. I salute; go through the whole military routine.

'PFC Wharton we think we have an assignment for you.'

'Yes Sir.'

We're playing the whole thing out. He reaches down into a drawer and pulls out a portfolio filled with papers and plastic overlays.

'I understand you had top marks in map reading and map making back at Jackson.'

He smiles at me and lights a cigarette. Damn, I'm still at attention, he hasn't even put me at ease. I wonder if I should just go into 'at ease' by myself. This jerk probably wouldn't even notice. Then again, maybe he's got a message from that bone doctor at the hospital and he's about to pull some kind of wild bamboozle on me. I keep my mouth shut. I stay at attention. He must have read my mind.

'At ease, Soldier.'

I slump appropriately.

'Major Love feels we ought to have a map of this town and the surrounding territory. It's good military procedure to be prepared. One never knows. Those Nazis are capable of anything, look at that guy Hess who practically jumped down the queen's chimney. He had to *give* himself up; these Limeys could never have caught him.'

I don't say anything. To be honest, I don't even know about Hess. I'm not very political. This war to me is something like whooping cough or measles you try to get through, or maybe more like chicken pox where you aren't supposed to scratch or you'll have big craters all over your face and body. I'm trying my damnedest not to scratch.

He reaches across the desk and hands me the portfolio. This is about to be one of the weirdest things to happen to me so far. Little did I know how weird things can get in the army. I can feel it in my bones, especially in that calcaneus spur. Does he expect me to go out and make little drawings of all the houses in town? I tuck the folder under my arm and come to attention again, half way.

'What we need is a complete map showing locations of all buildings, and what they're being used for. Indicate the mills we're living in as barracks, show where the motor pool is located. Get in all the important roads and even the little paths. Show the distance from one place to another in yards. Try to do the whole thing to scale. If there are some details, make detailed maps of those parts. If possible, indicate the topography with elevations. You can work out the scale, too, but be sure to have a legend so the Major can quickly have an idea of the terrain. I've taken you off all other duties and here's a pass to get you around town without any trouble. Try to make yourself as inconspicuous as possible. If you need a map table, you can get one from supply, also anything else you might need.

'You got all that?'

I hardly know what he's talking about. However, having a pass to go anywhere I want to in town without being locked inside that mill is just fine with me. I nod vigorously.

'Yes Sir. I'll do my best.'

He salutes and I whip him back a good one and spin on my heels with the portfolio under my arm. I'm going to need some pencils and drawing pens but I don't want to screw anything up.

I stop outside at the orderly's desk and he has the pass. He also lets me have two 2B drawing pencils and, after some convincing, a black fountain pen. I figure I'll stroll around town and look for any kind of a stationery store with a real drawing pen and some India ink. I'll also need a ruler and maybe a T square. I'm deep into the map making business.

More than that, I'm now practically a tourist. I stroll up the hill to look at the town church, it's something I've wanted to see. On the way, two MPs jump out of doorways and start hassling me. I show them my magic pass and do everything but salute. I could be a Nazi spy who just counterfeited that pass and I'll bet those idiots'd let me by anyway.

Maybe Williams is right, nobody's doing much of a great job running this war. Hey, maybe I can do all these drawings and sell them to the Germans. They might give me a German discharge in exchange. I could work on my German, disappear in the Alps somewhere and nobody would know the difference. No, they'd get me. With my luck, some hot-shot American skier would discover me in my little hut on the side of the hill and turn me in.

The church door is locked, but just down the hill on the other side is a little combination newspaper stand and stationery shop. There's an old lady and a very pretty girl running it. As I move toward the pretty one, the old one blocks my way. She's surprised to see a soldier walking around in broad daylight. All these people must know we're here but there's some kind of agreement that we'll all pretend we don't see or know anything.

I try to explain what I want. The old lady is confused, but the young one steps forward. She has very dark hair and beautiful violet eyes. She pulls down some dusty boxes and there are crow quill pens, and engineering pens, great for map drawing, but I'd have bought split goose feathers from her. She also has some quality pink pearl erasers. This master spy does make mistakes once in a while.

She also brings out some rulers, wooden and

thick, twelve inch jobs and, miracle of miracles, a transparent T square.

All the time, I'm trying to work up a conversation. I can't tell them what I'm really doing, although they've probably figured it out faster than I did. So, I tell them I'm an artist and will be doing drawings around town to pass the time.

I think of an old film with Ronald Coleman where he wanders through the English countryside with a portable easel on his back singing, 'When a body meets a body coming through the rye'; I romanticised over that one for six months. It could be one of the influences that made me want to be an artist. Of course, he meets the most beautiful girl in his wanderings and she thinks he's 'God's gift to earth' because he can draw and paint.

I wonder if I can talk Taylor into letting me buy a portable easel instead of hauling a map table around. He said I should make myself inconspicuous. Maybe I could even wear civilian clothes, some old tweeds and a Sherlock Holmes cap with a bill. The English would never shoot me as a spy, or maybe they would. I've lost a lot of confidence in the people who make those kinds of decisions.

There's a great wooden combination paint box and easel in the window. I ask the price. It's just under ten pounds. Taylor could never get a requisition through even if he'd try. But I act as if I'm seriously considering it, all in the interest of security. I ask the young girl her name and she tells me its Miss Henderson. I look at her, pretending I'm Ronald Coleman.

'Might I call you Violet?'

She blushes and turns around. I figure I've blown it. What would Ronald Coleman have done?

Luckily I have a bit over ten pounds in my pocket, more than enough. I ask for a receipt. I'll need it to get my money back, if that's remotely possible. Then I remember, I forgot India ink. I ask. Without a word she turns and takes a bottle from one of the shelves. She twists the top open to check if it's dried up. It is. She opens three before she finds one that's okay. India ink is like that. It goes to seed or something and you have bits of black grit in ink plasma and there's no way you can make it flow through a pen, especially a crow quill pen or an engineering pen. It's very nice of her to check.

'Thank you, Miss Henderson. There's nothing worse than having black sand for ink.'

She looks at me with those violet eyes.

'My name is really Michelle. It's a French sounding name isn't it?'

'My name is William. I'm called Will by my friends. I hope I'll be seeing you again.'

She smiles, gives me my change, looks me in the eye.

'Perhaps William, you might need some more India ink.'

I begin walking around the town, measuring distances, counting buildings, taking notes, humming 'Coming Through the Rye', thinking about violet eyes. This is going to be one terrific assignment. I'm pacing from the church to the mayor's office, trying to keep count, when I see Michelle coming up the street. She has a small cloth basket with packages in it. I know, from my wandering around, that today's market day, the day when the farmers come in to sell the few things they can sell that aren't rationed. I look up and lose count. Michelle stops in front of me.

'What are you doing William? I see you marching up and down the streets marking things on your papers. You don't look to me as if you are doing any drawings.'

So, I confess. I'm probably giving away state secrets to an enemy spy who's been posted in this town for almost twenty years and has a secret radio in her bedroom. I like to meditate on her bedroom.

'I'm trying to make a map of the town. My officer thinks it would be a good idea, in case any Germans come charging over the hill we'll all know which way to run.'

She swings her bag around so she's holding it with two hands in front of her. She looks at me, inquisitively, the same way she did in the shop.

'Well, William, I'm quite sure there are maps in the council archives. I think they would let you use them for your work, if you asked. In fact, if you want, I'll ask. My uncle is a council member.'

She smiles and turns away. She's about five steps back up the hill when Ronald Coleman asserts himself.

'How can I find out if this would be possible. Where should I go, Michelle?'

'Come to the shop this afternoon. I will know by then.'

She continues on up the hill. I'm totally confused. I can't even come within a hundred of how many paces I'd done when we met. I wait until she's out of sight, then sneak up the hill to the church again. I start pacing anew. At the bottom of the hill (the whole town is on the side of a hill) is a wooden cattle fence with a cattle gate. I go through it and I'm out in open country. Everything is deep green. We have some fair-to-middling green in

Pennsylvania, but this green is the kind you expect to find in Ireland.

Taylor'd said I was supposed to give some idea of the surroundings for this town so I go through the gate, turn and march across fields to another rolling hill beside the town, from which I have a great view of the entire area with the church on top of the hill, the line of streets and all the little side streets crossing it and down to the fence. There are sheep in the fields. I figure the fence is to keep the sheep out of town. There are the same kinds of fences at the end of each side street. I spend the afternoon drawing the town, then inking in my drawing. I don't even go back to the mill for chow. I've bought some hard rolls and soft cheese at a shop and nibble on them as I draw. Boy, I'm really into being Ronald Coleman now. I keep repeating that part, 'if a body kiss a body, need a body cry'.

At about two thirty, I have my drawing done. There are some things I don't like about it, especially the big brick mill in the middle of the town on the other side of the street. It really stands out like a sore thumb. I probably shouldn't have put it in. But then that's what Taylor wants. This will show I've been working seriously if he asks to see what I've done.

I head back to the stationery store. Michelle is there alone, without the older lady. She smiles when I come in. She holds out a paper with old fashioned writing.

'Show this to the woman at the desk in the public library. She'll be expecting you.'

'Where is the public library? We've all been looking for things to read but no one knew of a library.'

'Do you know where the chemist shop is?'

'You mean the drugstore.'

'Yes, that's right, what you call a drugstore. Well, just before you go into the chemist's, beside his door is a smaller door. It doesn't have any sign over it. You go up those stairs and knock on the door at the top. As I said, she's expecting you. There should be no problem and I think you will find all you want.'

I want to show her the drawing I've done in the field but instead buy another pink pearl eraser I don't need. I do make a lot of mistakes but not enough to wear out an eraser in one afternoon. She smiles her magic smile again.

'Thank you for everything, Miss Henderson. This could certainly save me much measuring and pacing around town.'

She looks quickly over her shoulder.

'You may call me Michelle or even Violet whichever you prefer, when we're alone. Mama is always
afraid I'll become too close with our American
friends.'

Another smile. I try a 'knowing' Ronald Coleman
smile of my own and back out of the store, almost
knocking over a whole stand of fountain pens in
the window stand by the door.

I find the library just as she said. The lady is
waiting for me there. I show her the note from
Michelle. She looks at it briefly, smiles, then turns
back into the room. The library couldn't have
more than a thousand books plus some periodicals,
also what I guess one could call the 'archives'. It's
to this part she goes, pulls out three cardboard
folders and comes back to the small narrow, shelf-
like counter separating us. The counter is hinged
so one can lift it to go in and out of the 'library'.
She unties the small string on the portfolio wrap
around ties, and opens it. I know this is it, all
right. I've struck gold. Somebody in the past has
done beautiful topographical maps of the town
and surrounding area. It even has contour lines
and is all to scale. I stare appreciatively at the
drawing. It is done with more loving care and
skill than I could ever manage, but is exactly what
I need. I smile up at the librarian.

'Would it be all right with you if I make copies of this? My officer at the mill wants maps of the town for defence purposes.'

She looks at me and smiles. Then her face purses. 'Yes, but you must not take these maps out of the library. It is not permitted. You would need to work on them here.'

That's fine with me. I have no desire to try making adequate copies either in the mill with that bunch of animals or out in the field.

'Would it really be possible, Madame? If so, I'd very much appreciate it.'

She lifts the hinged counter so I can come through. She clears off a library-type table of some books.

'Would this be a large enough place for you to work?'

I assure her it's more than I can possibly expect. She moves the folders onto one corner of the table and I spread my portfolio with my equipment.

I work the rest of the afternoon without interruption. Virtually no one comes into the library. It might be public but the public doesn't seem to know about it, use it. In America I'd figure it for a 'bookie' joint or a tax dodge of some kind.

The other maps are just as good as the first. One set shows all the various activities in the different buildings and the dates of construction. The other set shows the name of each person or organisation in every building as well as an indication of the type of surface on each of the roads or paths.

I decide to combine all three maps into one. With my overlays it's no big deal at all. With tracing paper, I make my first copy, then use this to make an ink 'original'. With this kind of work I'll really have something to show when I finish. I can spread this job out for weeks, that is, if we stay around that long. Maybe I'll even do such a beautiful set of maps I'll be assigned out of I&R into S2 proper, or even up to G2. That thought alone is enough to keep me working.

It's after five thirty on the big wooden wall clock when the librarian says she must close. She says it in such a way I feel she thinks she's interfering with the war effort by throwing me out. She hasn't come near me all day. Maybe she's afraid she'll see something secret she shouldn't see.

'Would it be all right if I left my drawings here in the library?'

'Certainly, do you think they would be quite safe?'

'It would be most convenient for me. Could you tell me what time you will be open tomorrow?'

She repeats a well-rehearsed, oft given, answer.

'We are open from nine to twelve and two to six every day, except Sunday. On Saturday we stay open all day from nine to six. Sundays we are closed. But, if you prefer, you may come here to work any time you want. I shall give Michelle Henderson the keys and she can let you in.'

This is getting better than I could have dreamed. Ronald Coleman would be proud of me. I take along some of the tracings I've done so I can show them to Taylor if he asks what I've been doing. I decide to keep the sketch from outside town for myself.

So it goes. Every day I go to work on that nice little library table. I really feel out of the army. I'm getting some terrific information and drawings. I couldn't *be* more inconspicuous. I don't think three people in town even know I'm doing any drawings. But Michelle still doesn't come around. I stop by the store once to buy some India ink but only her mother is there. She's nice to me, but I figure it's best not to ask about Michelle. She gives me my ink without checking to see if it's dry but when I get to the library it's perfectly okay. I was hoping for an excuse to go back.

In the mill, everybody's wondering where I've been, what I've been doing. They've made new mattresses from straw and burlap. Those guys are going stir crazy. There are about ten thousand rumours swirling around about what's going to happen. There are full days of close order drill, rifle practice and bayonet practice going on in the courtyard. Boy did I luck out.

Then Sunday comes. But, naturally, the stationery store is closed. I'm just turning around when the window over the store front opens and there's Michelle leaning over the sill. She holds out the key.

'I'll be right down. Mama is off to church.'

She comes down a flight of steps similar to those leading up to the library. She looks even more beautiful, not dressed in the sort of apron she wears in the shop. I try not to stare. She looks away from me, and we start up the street. It's amazing how quiet a little town in the Midlands can be on Sunday during a war.

She leads me up the stairs to the library and lets me go in first. I'm afraid for a moment she won't come in but she does, and locks the door behind her.

'Let me see what you have been doing all this time. Mama says you came to buy more ink when I was not there, so you must be doing something, or else you spilled it.'

I open and show her my combination maps. They are something of which I'm proud. She leans over them and I come up beside her. She has a smell of strong soap and no perfume. She seems so fragile, so beautiful to me; but then I guess anything female would have seemed so to me right then.

She must feel me leaning over her because she suddenly straightens up. She looks at me.

'Roger would really appreciate this. He is our school master and was asked to make all these maps two years ago before he went away. He hated making them, insisted he was a literary scholar and not some kind of artist. It is his mother who runs our library you see and these are all his books. It was his idea; he wanted the town and his former students to have access to a library easily, without having to go all the way to Congleton or Hanley. He loved reading and was such a fine person.'

So I've been told where I stand. It's a challenge even for Ronald Coleman. Nothing like this happened in the movie, but then, before I can move she looks me in the eye. I smile back at her. It's some kind of mind reading act. She must know I only came over to the store as an excuse to see her. My 'Ronald Coleman' act didn't fool her.

After about an hour's work, during which I try to tell her about the drawing I've done of the town from up on the hill, she's ready to leave. As she is about to go she turns back.

'Up there where you made your drawing, there is the best view around, and it is a lovely day, perhaps we could take a little picnic together.'

I nod, stupidly, very un-Ronald Coleman-like and we smile. She says she'll pack us a little to eat in a picnic basket and agrees to meet at the sheep gate by eleven o'clock. Her mother will be coming home by twelve thirty.

Well, I don't get much work done the rest of that morning. I'm watching the clock on the wall and sometimes it seems to be stuck. But finally, eleven arrives. The minute hands have been jumping in tiny clicks until they are at five minutes to eleven and I'm free. I lock up the library and head toward the sheep gate, trying not to hurry or run. Ronald Coleman would stride down the street very confident in himself. I am not.

She's already there. She's wearing the same clothes as this morning except for a blue green shawl over her shoulders. She smiles when she sees me and looks in all directions.

'I was afraid you would not come. I was so frightened, I almost did not come myself.'

'How could I not come? I watched the clock all morning.' We're both somewhat embarrassed. On top of the hill, Violet spreads out a blanket for our table cloth. She makes sandwiches from brown bread and a soft cheese. It's so great not to be eating GI food.

I pull out the first drawing I made, and she's most appreciative, pointing out different houses and saying who lives in them. We're more or less leaning against each other as we huddle over the drawing. Maybe war is worth it. I'd never have gotten to meet Violet.

After we've eaten and put things back in the basket, Violet looks at me, my heart almost stops. Our eyes can't escape. She puts out her hand. I cover it with mine. She starts, stops, then starts again. There are tears in her eyes.

'William, there is something I must tell you.'

She takes a deep breath.

'The man who made those drawings, Roger, is the man I am going to marry. We are not officially engaged because in my mother's eyes I am too young, but we have promised ourselves to marry when he comes back.'

She stops, looks down, away from my eyes, then looks up again.

'I am sorry, William. I thought you ought to

know. I enjoy your company very much and feel strongly toward you. I will miss you terribly when you are gone, but I do love Roger, you can see from his maps he is such a wonderful person.'

I'm sure Ronald Coleman would know exactly what to do, but I definitely don't. I sit there quietly. I can't look into her eyes or I'll cry. She reaches into the bottom of her picnic basket and pulls out a small sealed envelope.

"William, here is the address of a very good girlfriend of mine. She will give me any letters you send. I promise to write back. Is that all right?"

There's no way I can say 'no it isn't'. I promise. I tell her I'll write her from wherever I am.

She stands and I stand with her. We walk back to the sheep gate. We don't talk. At the gate, we stop and stare for a long moment into each other's eyes. Each of us is on the edge of tears. I'm embarrassed. What kind of Ronald Coleman am I? I don't ever remember him crying in any film. She hands me the envelope and runs away up the hill. I stand watching her.

We're shipped out to the coast two days later. I never see Violet again. I don't finish the maps; I turn them in to Major Love. I'm sure they don't mean anything any more to anybody.

I don't write to her and she doesn't write to

me. I have no real address to give her and I've lost her envelope with the address of her girlfriend. Much later I receive a short note through Regimental Headquarters from Violet with no return address. Roger has been killed in the air war over Britain. She doesn't want to live. She's happy she knew me for our brief time. Still I can't write. I tear everything apart looking for that envelope with the letter but it's gone. I've lost the address. In a war it is difficult to hold onto personal things.

D-3

We left Biddulph just as quickly and silently as we arrived. We hadn't been there a month when the order to move out came through. It was two days of getting everything in order and we left in the night on trains again. We all knew, in general, what we were going to do but none of us knew when or where, not even field officers knew as well as all the non-coms and enlisted men being kept in the dark. And when we arrived, we were literally in the dark. There didn't seem to be any moon and the clouds made it even darker. We get out of the trains, and, of course, are told to pitch tents. Pitching tents in the dark on an open field is a good trick. I'm tenting with Gettinger, who has taken Corbeil's place. He makes a good tent mate, doesn't snore or roll around too much. Also, he's one of those rare people who seem to fall asleep as soon as they stretch out. I'm definitely not that way, but I try not to twist and turn. A pup tent is a very small place for two grown men. Luckily neither Gettinger nor I is very big.

Three days after we arrive, we start beach landing maneouvres with the Landing Ship Infantry, called LSI and the Landing Ship Tanks, called LST. It's the beginning of summer but in England it's still cold and the water is icy. We slog through that cold water, looking out at the white cliffs above the beaches, trying to keep our rifles dry and hoping that France doesn't have any cliffs like those. Getting our clothes dry each day is another problem. Half the time it's raining. We only have two pair of OD trousers and shirts plus our field jackets. As far as I can see, we are all going to have pneumonia before the Germans even have a chance to shoot at us. It's strange to be camping so close to the enemy and having it be so quiet. At night we can hear the planes flying over and there are huge balloons all along the coast. It doesn't look as if anybody is really trying to keep a secret about what's going on, except from us.

Now begins an experience that I not only didn't tell my children, but I've told no one but my wife. In this particular set of events, I not only behave like the young fool I was, but I'm set up with a situation which is so incredible, I didn't believe it then or even understand it now.

It all starts with a command car rolling through our little tent city just after chow. I'm finishing up some fruit cocktail dumped over the last bit of my mashed potatoes and hash. There's too long a line at the clean up pail to wait around again. It all comes together in my stomach anyway. I'll clean up my mess kit after everybody's finished.

It seems the Lieutenant in the command car driven by a Staff Sergeant is looking for *me*. I don't know what to expect, maybe they've changed their minds about sending a cripple with varicose veins in his balls and a lump on his heel into combat. I couldn't have been more wrong.

It's the first time I've been in a command car. They're certainly a lot roomier than a jeep. I have the entire back seat to myself. I wave to Gettinger and some other guys as I roll along, weaving our way through the tents. They don't wave back, only stare.

We go about three miles, always away from the beach. It's looking good. Then we come to a big house. There are armed guards all around this place, even up the pebble driveway to the front. We stop. The Lieutenant motions me to follow him. Now I'm worried. What could they have possibly cooked up for me. I hope it isn't a court martial for something I've overlooked. No, it wouldn't be something small like that. This is big.

I've just gotten out of the command car when I realise I've forgotten my rifle; I was eating when they came. At least I have on my helmet. We're supposed to wear those heavy pots on our heads no matter what we're doing; even in the tent, we're supposed to keep them near our heads when we sleep.

I follow the Lieutenant into the house. It's a regular house with furniture and rugs, actually a very fancy place to be in the middle of a war. The Lieutenant still hasn't said a word to me. It isn't a good idea to start up a conversation with a Lieutenant, so I don't, that's his job.

Finally we go into a big room. I can see it was once a library. There are books all along the walls. Huge windows going down to the floor are blacked out. It's still light outside but the lights are turned on in here. The Lieutenant shows me where to sit in a chair along the wall and then leaves. There are three officers around a huge desk in the middle of the room. They're all looking down at something. At first, I can't see it, but then one of them motions me forward. I stand at attention and salute. He gives me a careless salute back.

'At ease, Soldier.'

I go into my personal version of 'at ease.' I peek down at the desk. What they're looking at are my drawings of the maps I did in Biddulph. What now? Are we going to invade England? I'm beginning to be scared because I don't understand.

'Soldier, you're the one who did the maps for the town of Biddulph here?'

It's definitely a question. I nod, then pull myself together.

'Yes, Sir. They were ordered by Major Love.'

I'm wondering if they've found out how I copied them from the maps in the library. Could that be some kind of military offence?

'These are very good maps. I see from your records you've also been exceptionally good using the 506 radio and can take Morse code. Is that correct?'

What are we getting at. Maybe I'll be transferred to G2 doing some kind of secret work.

'Yes Sir. In high school, in a class before school, I learned it. We did it in the typing room and typed out messages from records. I wasn't particularly good at it, but neither was anyone else.'

'It says here you typed at sixty-two words per minute and took code even faster than that.'

I don't really remember. I took the class for fun because our bus always arrived early and the principal of our school would set up anything to help the 'war effort'. They don't need to know that.

'That's right, Sir. I don't know how fast I could do it now because I haven't had much practice.'

'That's all right.'

He pauses, starts talking to the officer beside him. It's then I notice he's a bird colonel, the same as our Regimental Commander, but I've never seen him before. He turns back to me.

'Soldier, you're also in Regimental Intelligence and Reconnaissance and you have had jump training at Fort Benning. Is that right?'

He has to know this. It's in my service record and I can see it on the desk right beside the map. I decide to keep my mouth shut. The rule we've been told is when we've been captured we give only our name, rank and serial number. I've been captured here all right. Maybe these are Nazi spies who have gotten hold of US equipment and uniforms. I decide that's ridiculous. They wouldn't call me in. But then, I've already seen some ridiculous things in the army.

'We have a mission for you, Soldier, a special

kind of patrol. Your record as a patrol leader is also good.'

I wait, my heart literally in my mouth. How can we have a patrol when we aren't even in combat yet?

'This mission must remain top secret, Soldier. You're not to mention it to anyone. Don't talk about it to any of the members in your regiment. Do you understand me?'

I don't, really, but I nod my head.

'It is a very important mission. We can't force you to do it, but you are the best candidate.'

Now, he has my attention full out. I try not to keep my mouth from opening.

'There will be three different invasions going up those beaches over there. One is the American, then the British and the other, Canadian. We'll all be going in at the same time in very close formation, wave after wave. Do you understand?'

I do, but I don't want to. This is not something they should be telling a mere PFC. Crazy as the army is, this is too much.

'We want to drop you by parachute behind the main German defences. There is something of no-man's land there. The rest of the German defensive forces have been driven back by our long range artillery.'

He pauses. I wait for him to go on. This all sounds like a very poor movie. Where's Van Johnson, John Wayne? All 4F, I guess. They know how to do these things. I just stand there waiting.

'Are you willing to serve your country, young man?'

What would happen if I say no? But I say yes, a small, almost inaudible, 'yes'.

'Congratulations. If you succeed I shall see to it that you are awarded at least a silver star. Do you understand?'

He's staring me in the eyes again. That almost inaudible 'yes' must have tipped him off. I didn't even say Sir.

He looks over his shoulder. He nods one of the other officers forward.

'Major McGeehan here will explain the patrol to you. If you don't think you can do it, you can always back out. Nobody will hold it against you. Got that, Soldier?'

I got it all right, basically no way out. I stand there as Major McGeehan rolls out some other maps over mine. He motions me forward. I come and look down at the maps. They're not as good as mine, but then, after all, I cheated.

'You see we're here. The British are there and the Canadians are there. When we have some reasonable weather and the supreme commander gives the word, we take off for these beaches here.'

He points with his fingers to the coast of France. I don't really know one part of France from the other, no one's mentioned it.

I only nod. He doesn't look up. He starts making arcs with his fingers on the maps.

'These are the general areas of penetration for each group but you don't want to know too much detail. You might be captured and we want the enemy to know as little as possible.'

I'm wondering how those Germans can capture me. Are they about to invade England? Nobody's said anything about that. We aren't even dug in, just splashing around in the water, sleeping in wet clothes and being miserable. Only then I realise they're going to capture me in France! I'm ready to quit.

'You will be driven from here to a small airfield not far away. From there in the dead of night, actually early morning, you will be flown over the Channel.'

He points out the so called no-man's land, then pulls out another map. It's a photographic blow up.

'This was taken by our aerial reconnaissance team. You can see there's a large tree which was blown down here in our artillery barrage.'

He points to a blurred smudge on the map. I peer. What's this got to do with anything?

'A small plane will drop you with a black parachute near this tree in the dark.'

He smiles at me as if he's a magician who has just pulled a rabbit out of a hat.

'You will be carrying a combat pack filled with K rations, enough for several days. On your chest will be strapped a radio well padded for the impact of landing. Of course you will also have the parachute which will be hanging low. On your webbing belt will be a small pistol.'

So, with this pistol I'm supposed to fight off the entire German army? How can I get out of this? I don't really want to be a hero; in fact I'm not sure we should even win this war. I'm willing to learn German.

'You must be very careful with your landing. You must land on your back holding your arms around the radio. The radio is the most important thing.'

I look at him to see if he's kidding. He isn't.

'Then after you've landed, and you're okay, you gather in the chute and dash to the shelter in the roots of this tree. This will need to be done quickly because there's a chance someone might have seen you coming down.'

He's serious. I can't believe it. He's got the wrong guy. They must have made a terrible mistake.

'You're to spread out the chute in the hole left by the roots. Cover yourself with the parachute as night camouflage and get the radio operating. Try to make contact with us or our allies. Warrant Officer Mullen will tell you which frequencies to search.'

He stops, looks at me again.

'Any questions?'

'How do I get out of there, and when?'

'There will be French Freedom Fighters, "Les Maquis", with whom we are in contact who will be watching for you. They know where you're being dropped and they'll help you if the invasion is delayed for any reason.'

'What am I supposed to be doing there? I still don't understand.'

'You have several missions. At first, you will be trying to get in contact with the British and the Canadians, as well as the Americans to assure them that they won't veer and begin shooting at each other in the dark. There is always that possibility in a situation such as this. Next, as soon as possible, you will deliver the radio to the French. They know what to do with it. They'll take care of you and help you get out. Don't worry, Warrant Officer

Mullen will explain all this in more detail to you.'

He stops, looks at his watch, his job is finished, I'm totally confused. He leans across the desk and shakes my hand.

'Good luck, Soldier. The driver is outside and will take you back to your outfit so you can gather up your things. You won't need your helmet, rifle, bayonet or any M1 ammunition. Warrant Office Mullens will provide you with all you will need. Remember, you're not to say a word about anything you've heard here, or about your mission. We're counting on you.'

On some kind of cue, the driver comes in to pick me up. The Lieutenant isn't in the command car. I sit up front with the Sergeant and go over in my mind all that's happened in the past hour or two. I almost begin to think I'm going crazy, or this is some kind of joke and tomorrow everybody will have a big laugh out of it.

We arrive at our tent city and he drives off. We haven't spoken a word. I come back to my tent and it's almost dark. Gettinger wants to know what it's all about.

'Stan, if I told you, you wouldn't believe it. I can hardly believe it myself. Don't ask too many questions. My head is spinning so I have a headache.' He rolls over, and, as usual, is directly asleep. I pack my few things in my duffel bag and deliver them to the kitchen truck. I'll leave my shelter half, pole and pegs with Stan. I feel like a husband sneaking out of a marriage, but with no lover to greet me.

The command car is there just after breakfast. I wash the eggs out of my mess kit, stuff the mess kit into my duffel bag, shoulder it and am off, way off. We drive for almost an hour, this time along the beach when we can stay close to it. It's the same Staff Sergeant and we have just about as much conversation as before, that is, none. Maybe he's a guy with a hearing deficiency who the army keeps to drive people like me on suicide missions.

We arrive at a small airport. The Sergeant motions for me to stay in the car and goes into a hangar. In a few minutes he comes out and motions me to pick up my gear and go in. I struggle out of the command car, the last one I ever get driven in, and go into the hangar.

Inside is a Warrant Officer. He introduces himself as Pat Mullens. A warrant officer is between a commissioned officer and a non-commissioned officer, sort of a limbo in officialdom. Usually warrant officers have some technical speciality. I can see Officer Mullens' speciality behind him. It's a small airplane painted a dark mottled grey not olive drab like most army equipment. He takes me into a little office behind the plane. He moves a chair for me to sit in; no ordinary officer would ever do that.

'Look, Wharton, this is the craziest mission I've ever heard of. I'm not the one who thought it up. I've heard all kinds of things, but from what I hear it's some high ranking staff officer who got the idea, but he doesn't want anyone to know who he is. How do you like that for army secrecy? You and I are going on a mission neither one of us knows anything about.'

My heart jumps a beat.

'You mean you're coming with me?'

'Well, I'll be flying you across the Channel.'

'But I've only been in an airplane one time in my life and that was when I was six years old. My father paid five dollars for the two of us to have a ride in a two winger, a biplane, at Wilson Airfield in Philadelphia. I was scared to death we were going to fall out. So was my father. There was no strap or anything to hold us in.'

'One of those old Barnstormers, I guess. Well, we'll be flying in little *Sally* there, but we won't be going very high. You did do five jumps at Fort Benning, didn't you?'

'Yeah, but that was different. It was daytime and we were all hooked together. I didn't exactly jump. I was pulled out and the chute opened by itself.'

'This will be different. We'll go across the Channel only about ten feet above the water. We don't want them to see us. When the time comes, after I've gotten some altitude, I'll just tip the plane and you'll slide right out. You'll need to pull your own ripcord the minute you're out of the plane.'

'What's a ripcord?'

He looks at me as though he's just seen me.

'I'll show you. Come follow me and we'll set everything up.'

I go out with him to the airplane. It has a top wing, no bottom one, like the Taylor Cubs I used to see down at Wilson Airport when I'd bicycle down there as a kid. We walk into the depths of the hangar. The Warrant Officer walks ahead of me. He has everything ready, all the way down to heavy gloves, a jump suit and a parachute. I stare at them.

He looks at me.

'Are you sure you want to do this? We can always back out of it you know. I'm pretty sure I can get you there, but the rest, I don't know.'

This, for sure, is where I should have opted out. I know now, I was caught up in the great male double bind. For one thing, all the preparations, the expectations, it seemed to have a real life of its own. For another, it was in the same category as any risky, fascinating challenge such as skiing, driving a car fast, all of it. I'm stupidly challenged. At first, I'm interested in just how I'm to be dressed for this patrol, what kind of costume, like a football player, I would be wearing. In many ways I'm still a child, no question.

He's even rigged a way for me to carry that heavy radio across my chest. He picks up the jump suit from the seat of his plane and holds it out to me, watching to see what I'll do. I take it, try it on. It fits. They must have my measurements filed somewhere. I pull up the zippers, snap all the snaps; he helps me with this. Then he lifts the radio from the back of the plane. It's all wrapped in blankets to cushion it and keep dirt out, I presume. He lifts it and settles it on cushioned braces over my shoulders, tightening it down. It settles on my chest and he straps it down around me. He pulls out a leather cap, the kind old time aviators used to wear and fits it on my head, snaps that. He reaches into the plane again and pulls out a webbing belt with a knife and pistol on one side and a double canteen (two strapped together) on the other. He steps back to look at me.

'You look something like a deep sea diver. Let's

hope that will not be the case. You know I didn't work all this gear out. There were two other WOs and a T4 who came in with this equipment and rigged it up. I'd never seen them before.'

'I'm getting hot in this crazy outfit. Is it okay if we take it off now?'

'Sure.'

He starts unbuckling and unstrapping me. I help him with the zippers. It feels good to wiggle out of the whole rig. I'm scared but it's hard to be really scared of something you know nothing about.

'Sir, what do you know about this patrol? It sounds impossible to me.'

'Don't Sir me. Call me Pat. We're in this together.'

'I'm Will.'

'Okay, this is what I know. I'm to fly out of here, cross three miles north, flying about ten feet above the water, depending on how rough the channel looks. I'm to display no lights, which is going to make this quite a maneouvre in this dark. Before we go, we'll need to sit in total darkness here to get rid of the visual purple in our eyes so we can see at all. Then we'll start off.

'Those technician guys have put special mufflers on poor *Sally* so she hardly makes any noise at all. I've experimented flying with them and she loses a lot of power, but she's quiet. I'll need to top off my gas tanks to make it across and back because she's not so fuel efficient this way.'

He stops. I watch his face. He's sweating. I was in that hot suit and *he's* sweating.

'The problem is going to be picking just the right place to rev her up fast so I can make five hundred feet, go into an almost stall, and tip you out.'

He takes a deep breath and looks down at his feet.

'So, what do you know, Will?'

'I'm not supposed to tell anybody about this, but since you're in it too with me, it's probably okay.'

'I'm supposed to land, protecting the radio, bundle up the chute, then hide in a tipped up, bombed out tree where the roots have left a hole. From there I'm supposed to scan all the bands with the radio, especially three bands I've been given. I'm not supposed to broadcast, so the Germans won't have a chance to triangulate on me. Then, some French Freedom Fighters are supposed to come for the radio and get me out of there. I don't know how. I don't think I'm *supposed* to know how.'

'Jesus H. Christ! That's wild. Sure you don't want to back out?'

'I'm not sure of anything. I'm still *thinking* about it.'

'Well, you have about eight hours to make up your mind. I've been told they're going to hold up on artillery in the landing zone for one hour between three and four in the morning. I guess if we get you down and in there safely, they'll hold off longer.'

He puts his hands on his hips, then starts stuffing the jump suit, radio and the rest in the plane.

'Oh yes, I'm supposed to show you these.' He pulls out a full box of K rations, padded and strapped the way the radio is. 'I'll drop this just after I tip you out. They should land near you.'

'You're really going to just tip me out?'

'That's what I'm supposed to do. See, I've taken the door off on your side. With all that equipment and the jump suit you could never get out on your own.'

I wonder why I don't just call it off right there. I'm scared enough. But that's all past now. I'm in for it.

At half past two, I'm dressed, strapped up and in the plane. Herb's in the pilot's seat. A soldier, who came out of the depth of the dark hangar, twists the propeller, and on the third twist, it starts. Pat has a little half steering wheel to guide the plane and a joystick between his legs.

As a kid I'd sent in some box tops and received a small booklet from Little Orphan Annie or Bobby Benson, I forget which, that was supposed to show me how to fly an airplane. I'd practise down in the cellar using the top of a broom as my 'joystick'. Mom came down and asked me what I was doing. I told her I was playing with my 'joystick', learning how to fly. She was mad at first, but when she saw the directions for flying I was reading she went upstairs.

It's great to see a *real* joystick. Pat has his hand on it, but mostly he's pushing pedals with his feet and steering. We speed down the runway and rock a little when we leave the ground. I look out that open door. We're going fast and the ground seems to be sliding away under us. I decide not to look. We take off out over the water. I can just pick out the small flecks of waves as we go over them. We've steadied some and I'm not so afraid of falling out but I hold onto what looks like the dashboard of a car.

I don't know how long it is we fly, and Pat's concentrating to keep us in the air and not in the water. Sometimes there are bumps of some kind and he needs to adjust for them. The water is getting rougher and it's cold. I'm glad for the jump suit and gloves.

When we see the French coast he turns toward me.

'I'm going up a bit to fly over the German defensive positions. They can't see us soon enough, or fast enough, to ever hit us but it's best to be safe.'

I can pick out what look like concrete houses. Pat tells me these are built in bunkers. Then we come to what look like empty space. There are no lights. Pat turns to me.

'I'm going to go up as steep as I can until I almost stall, then I'll tilt your way and you'll slide out. Don't forget to hold onto and pull that ripcord. Try to land on your feet and fall backward keeping your arms ahead of you wrapped around that radio.'

Quickly, the plane is going almost straight up and is slowing. He tilts, and, before I know it, I'm out and in the air! I pull the ripcord, and it seems forever before the chute opens. Then I'm swinging back and forth and the land is coming up to me fast. I bunch myself over forward. It isn't two minutes later when I hit. My legs almost fold under me but I go backwards, holding onto the radio. Then I black out in the dark.

I have the wind knocked out of me and can't get my breath. I slowly roll over onto my knees. The chute is catching air and pulling me toward it. It pulls me over on my side. I'm still trying to get some air in my lungs, at the same time pulling with the guidelines of the chute to bring it toward me. It takes all the strength I have left. When I finally feel the black chute in the dark, I flop out on it to hold it down. I lie there listening and trying to breathe. I don't hear anything but my own hard breathing. From the ground, I can just pick out the roots of that big twisted tree against the sky.

Crawling on my knees, I pull the rest of the chute and pack it close against my chest, over the radio. I stand and start running toward the tree.

The hole is deep enough and I slide down the muddy side. It's about there I remember the box with the rations. I'm not exactly hungry, but if somebody finds it out in this seemingly open field, they'll look for me.

I unstrap myself from the chute, which comes up between my legs and over my shoulders. Then I lift off the radio. After those straps are undone, it's easy to shuck it off by leaning forward so it slides to the ground. It should hold the parachute down. I'm still breathing hard. I'm scared to death and my hands are shaking so badly I have a hard time releasing myself from all the straps. I decide to keep the jump suit on for now, although it's all sweated up. My face is cold.

I slide up to the edge of the hole and peer around for the rations. I think I see the box off to the left of where I came down. I creep over toward it looking all around me as I go. I don't take the pistol out. I find the rations and drag them along behind me holding on by one of the straps. I pull them down in the hole with me. I'm absolutely pooped.

I should unwrap the radio and start searching the bands, but I'm out of steam. I guess this is combat; I haven't heard a shot or seen anybody, but I'm a nervous wreck. Some kind of soldier I'm going to make. What'll I do if I ever need to duck small arms fire or hide down in a hole during an artillery bombardment. I hate to think about it.

I spread the parachute around in my little tree hole to cover up as much mud as I can feel. I look at my watch and it's almost five o'clock. It's June, so the sun will be up soon. I stretch out on my parachute with its pouch for a pillow and I'm out before I know it. I didn't have any sleep the whole night before from worrying and normally I'm asleep by ten or ten thirty at the latest. I'm definitely in the wrong business.

When I wake, it's two o'clock in the afternoon. I'd slept nine hours. Except for my sore back and the sore backs of my arms, I'm in reasonable shape. It's raining and some of the rain is seeping into my hole. I gather up rocks and build a dam across to help keep the hole dry and the rain out.

Next, I unwrap the radio and hope it will work. It looks okay. When I toggle the switch, it lights up and I start cruising the bands I've memorised where I'm supposed to call, but I'm getting nothing. The temptation is to put in a short broadcast myself so they'll know I'm okay, but I resist. I pull the antennae to its maximum length but still nothing. I'm hungry.

I crack open the provisions but it's only boxes of K rations. I open a lunch ration with the cheese, cracker, candy and the cigarettes I have no use for. I gnaw on the cheese and try to settle my stomach. I wonder how long I'll be out here alone.

Maybe they've already started the invasion and I don't even know it. Maybe they've decided to call it off, after all.

The food settles me down. I mix some of the Nescafé powder in some cold water from one of my canteens. The canteen is inside a fitted cup so I fill the cup about half with water. I'm thinking of water rationing already. The powder just turns into a sticky gum. It's supposed to be used with hot water. But by constantly swishing it around with my finger it finally starts to dissolve. I drink it but it's worse than water alone. I won't try that again.

When I'm finished eating, I scan the bands one more time, hoping for the best. Still nothing. I try other bands and all I get is what sounds like Germans talking. Just *that* scares me. I settle back and decide there's not much I can do. I peer out from my hole and in the misting rain can't see anything but a bombed out field. Nothing is alive in it, not even grass. I'd like to set up a guard but I'd be the only one on guard duty and that wouldn't work very well. I'll just need to keep a watch on things.

I decide I'll try the radio every hour on the hour. It sounds like something a real radio operator would do. I'll try not to sleep in the daytime. At nights I know I can't stay awake, but with the bumpiness of this hole, rocks and everything, I won't sleep much. I'll take a look around every time I wake and do another search with the radio. I'm wondering where the French Freedom Fighters are and when they'll arrive. I assume they know I'm under this uprooted tree. But maybe I'm assuming too much. I build another two rows of rocks along the perimeter of the hole and pack them with dirt. I'm not only better protected from the wind and rain, but I have more space, less rocks to sleep on. I've taken the pistol and the canteens along with the webbing belt off and have them in a dry high place, hanging on one of the roots of the tree. I hope I don't need to use that pistol. I won't. If Germans find me, I'm just going to give up. I can't fight off the entire German army myself. I don't want to even try.

I work out a regular routine. Every hour I turn on the radio and listen to the Germans talk. I can't do it for long because I'm afraid of wearing out the battery. Then I eat my K rations at seven in the morning, noon and six at night. I wind the watch while eating my dinner ration.

The weather lets up some. There are mixed clouds and sometimes a bit of sun shines through. France certainly has lousy weather for June. I haven't given up hope but I'm thinking about it. I know it would be suicide to try working my way back through the German defences, coming up on them from the rear. Those guys must be as nervous as cats; they wouldn't even give me a chance to think of surrendering. No, I'm stuck. I should never have gotten into this thing. My only chances are the Americans or British or Canadians breaking through to me, or those phantom French Freedom Fighters coming to my rescue for the radio. There's nothing to do but wait. I have enough rations for four days, after that, I'll need to do some thinking. I look down at myself. The jump suit is covered with mud. I look like something from a Flash Gordon movie when he'd go to some other planet in the twenty-fifth century.

The days go by. Nothing happens. I can hear the artillery pounding away all around me, but nothing much comes where I am. They've already pounded this stretch into virtual oblivion. I watch, scan with the radio, eat my rations, cat nap and wind the watch.

Three days go by. Then, out in front of me, I see some men moving in coming across the field. They have their rifles out and are in combat patrol formation, but running. How long do I wait? I strip off the jump suit to make myself look more like an American soldier. I take off my aviator's hat which has kept my ears warm. I can see from the helmets these are not Germans, but they don't look like American troops either.

I start yelling in English while I'm still down in my hole. I leave everything including the pistol, the radio and the rations. I come out of the hole with my arms out shouting *I'm an American! Don't shoot! I'm an American!!* They stop in their tracks. I stand and slowly walk toward them. They've dropped to their stomachs and have their rifles trained on me.

'Stop right there.'

I stop.

One of them comes toward me. I keep my arms over my head. We talk. He speaks English with an English accent, but it turns out they're Canadian troops. I show him my dog tags. He believes me. I take him forward to my hole.

'Jesus! You Yanks will try anything. Nobody told us you'd be out here.'

'French Freedom Fighters were supposed to come and get me, mostly for the radio I have in the hole there. Is there any way you guys can get me back to my outfit in England? I'm running short of rations.'

We work it out. He advises me to carry the pistol. The chute, jump suit and the remaining rations we leave in there. He asks me all kinds of questions about the situation here. They're moving blind. I can't tell him a thing, of course, except that I haven't seen anyone moving around here until they came.

He assigns one of his squad to take me back to the beach. It seems the invasion started three days ago. He says it was a 'bloody' affair and they thought they'd never really get a foothold but now things were a bit better. More and more troops were being landed. He said to watch out for mines. Also, there were still some German snipers holed up in some of the bunkers.

We make it through without any trouble. I still haven't been shot at that I know of. There are freight train-like artillery shells going over us but nothing coming down. At the beach it's like a military trash heap. Equipment is scattered every-where, even down into the water. Dead soldiers are sprawled all over the beach. Medics are running back and forth trying to move the wounded into the landing craft after they bring in new troops. It's hard to believe.

A Lieutenant, after being convinced by my guard and after I'd shown my dog tags, allows me to climb into one of the landing craft going back. Here, for the first time, I'm really under fire. The Germans are trying to stop the landing crafts, both coming in and going out. We have two shells explode at the sides of the boat. All those who aren't wounded duck over the wounded; and the sailors in charge of the boats are going as fast as they can out of there.

We reach a large ship, at last. The wounded are transferred out first, then I'm allowed to go aboard. The equivalent of an American SP takes me in charge. He holds me safe against a wall on deck while another SP goes forward. About five minutes later, we're ushered into a comfortable cabin with an English officer sitting at a map strewn desk. I explain the whole thing, as much as I know about it, to him. He keeps his head down until when I tell about jumping from the open door. He takes off his cap. He's bald.

'Extraordinary! So you say you've been out there in front of us for the past three days.'

'Four Sir, counting the day I came down.'

'Let me check this out. It's hard to believe.'

He pulls one of the phones on his desk toward him. He swivels his chair around so his back is to me. After about five minutes he turns back again and hangs up the phone.

'Soldier, you're being transferred to an American ship. A certain Colonel Munch wants to talk to you as soon as possible.'

'Yes, Sir.'

Orders are given, transport arranged, and quickly I'm aboard an American ship and being ushered into another well-furnished room. Sitting there is the Colonel who started this whole thing. He looks up at me, smiles.

'So, you're still alive.'

'That's right, Sir, I think.'

'What happened? Why didn't you get in touch with us? We've been scanning for your radio but could find nothing. One trouble was no one thought to register the code number of our equipment.'

'Yes, Sir. I called the bands I'd been given every hour on the hour but all I could find were Germans broadcasting. I'd been told not to broadcast because I would be triangulated and located.'

'My God, what a fuck up.'

I don't know whether he's referring to me, or the whole operation. I don't think I fucked up, but the entire operation was useless.

'Well Soldier, considering the situation, you did a good job. Did you get the radio to the Free French?'

'No Sir, they never came.'

'Where is it then?'

'I left it there, hoping they'd finally show up and find it. They must have known about that tree where I was hiding.'

He's looking down at his desk. He looks up at me.

'Do you have the watch?'

I unbuckle it and hand it to him.

He checks the time.

'Well, your outfit hasn't jumped off yet. It could be several weeks before the beachhead is widened enough to handle them. I'll get you back to them right away.'

He acts as if I should thank him. But I don't. He's a bit like that doctor with my varicocele and calcaneus spur. He's doing me a favour.

He puts out his hand and we shake. A sailor comes into the room.

'See that this man gets back to his outfit.'

He tells him the number of my regiment. We salute and I go with the sailor. No mention of my silver star.

I'm transported over three days back to my outfit in England. Gettinger still has my place reserved in the tent. I go gather up my duffel bag. Gettinger wants to know where I've been for the last week. I figure I might as well tell him. The mission is over, if not completed. He can't believe it any more than I can.

4. INVASION

SERGEANT BILLY DAN GRAY

We finally do get over. They've built temporary docks so we don't need to splash through the water. They've had the Saint Malo breakthrough so we've missed all the fighting in the hedgerows. None of us are complaining about that. We bivouac in an apple orchard and are told we'll be moving out soon.

We're all concerned because the village church has a rooster on top of the steeple where a cross should be. We're convinced the filthy, Godless Nazis have done this. Meanwhile, the people living around us are giving us bottles of what looks like apple cider. We're all drinking it from the bottle. Some of our more knowing members, our native Tennessee guys, tell us this is applejack and they're drinking it and falling all over the place. We, the

111

less knowing in the company, think it's just apple juice and are swilling it down until they pass on the word.

In the drunken mob we've become, we determine to take that Nazi rooster off the church and put a cross up there. One old timer buck sergeant convinces us all he had a job as a steeple jack in civilian life one time, and can get up to the top of the steeple. He points out a small door opening at the slanting top of the steeple, just under the rooster. We all join in this 'Christian' project. Someone finds the lock to the door up to the steeple and twists it off. Sergeant Billy Dan Gray takes the wooden cross somebody's carved and starts up to the top of the church staggering on the steps. We all go outside and watch. None of us would really be heartbroken if he falls. He's been making life miserable for his entire squad.

We watch as he climbs out of that small door way up there. Some villagers have gathered around to watch. One is a priest and he runs back and forth pointing up and babbling in French. He's obviously trying to understand what's going on.

Billy Dan climbs out of that little hole and, with his legs wrapped around the steeple, manages to hold onto the rooster and wind vane up there. He unhooks it somehow and throws it down to us.

It almost beheads Smitherson who is standing and watching. Billy Dan has the wooden cross stuck in his back pocket and pulls it out. He seems to be jamming it into the holder for the rooster and vane. He manages to get it pretty straight. Everybody gives him a big hand when the wooden cross is in place, except for the priest who has gathered up the rooster and vane and run away with them. We figure he must have been a Nazi sympathiser. So ends our little ignorant experience with French churches. I find out later that roosters are normal on churches in France.

Two days later we're packed into two ton trucks and start our tour across France following General Patton's tanks. We're headed for Paris.

HIDE AND SEEK

In the I&R, our major assignment is patrolling. Our patrols are usually reconnaissance searching out information. They are not attack or 'Tiger' patrols to take prisoners. The exception would be when we're asked to take a prisoner for interrogation. These are the worst jobs and we all dread them. Relative to line companies, most of the time in the regimental company we live an easy life, although we are in the field.

When we do go out it can be dangerous, serious, because we're usually sent into situations where it's felt that an ordinary platoon, company or even a battalion I&R patrol would not be adequate.

Our outfit moves quickly through most of France after Saint Malo, without too much resistance on our front. We bypass Paris. The French want to take it themselves. We continue through the rest of France, with the help of tanks, until we reach the French – German border.

Then, we're in the Saar valley. It's our first penetration into German territory. The regiment has been moving forward for over three weeks, but now we're bogged down in mud and stone-walled by at least two German Panzer divisions. Regimental headquarters is in a place called Olmsdorf. Just before midnight, on an early fall day, my new tent mate, Wilkins, and I are called into the Regimental Colonel's tent. My old tent mate, Gettinger, has been promoted to assistant squad leader for the Second Squad. Wilkins and I are the first and second scouts for the first squad of the first platoon. It would be impossible to make a worse choice for scouts.

We're dead asleep when Anderson, the I&R platoon Lieutenant, sticks his head in our tent and tells us to get over to the S2 tent on the double, the Regimental Commander wants to see us. It's as if God himself has come down to earth and summoned us.

The Colonel's tent is like the tent of a desert king. It has everything except Persian carpets and a hookah in the corner. There's a cot with a heavy sleeping bag, a map table, another table for eating, surrounded by camp chairs. The Colonel is wearing his long OD underwear with an OD towel over his head and his feet in a bucket of hot water. He blows his nose and looks up at us when we come into the tent. He looks into his OD handkerchief. He looks at a sheet of paper on the map table beside him, next to a large situation map. I figure he's looking to check our names.

'At ease men.'

We do the 'at ease' bit. I'm still sleepy. I realise I don't have my canteen or canteen holder, that makes me out of uniform. I used the canteen as a pillow and forgot it in our rush from the pup tent. There actually isn't much shortage of water, it's rained all day.

'Privates Wilkins and Wharton, we need a recon patrol going through Company B's forward outposts.'

He leans toward his map table. He seems so old to me, but he is probably only fifty. His liver spotted hand with thick fingers and clean finger-nails point to a spot on the map. He slides his fingers forward on the celluloid.

'At 0-five-thirty, we'll have corps artillery hit them with everything we've got. Then we'll move out at 0-six hundred. This is a penetration attack, a "feeler", just to see what's out there.'

He looks up at us, actually through us. He blows his nose again.

'But we don't want to go out there blind. There could be bunkers, tanks, who knows what else. We've had conflicting reports.'

I try not to look at Wilkins. How do *we* find out if there are tanks and bunkers without them finding *us*?

'Yes, Sir.'

Wilkins chimes in more slowly, with less enthusiasm. Maybe I'm still asleep and this is only a bad dream. I peer around the tent. Major Love, the S2, is there, and so is Major Collins, the Colonel's Adjutant. I see Lieutenant Anderson hovering, maybe hiding, inside the flap of the tent. This is a nightmare all right, but I'm not asleep. They're all watching us, two mere PFCs with quite an audience.

I'm feeling scared, over awed, uncomfortable with all this brass hanging over me. I pretend to listen as Love briefs us, but my mind is miles away. I'm considering everything from insubordination to desertion. I figure I did my part for the crazy war with that dumb D-3 day. Or maybe I could work up a quick section 8 by trying to float some cartridges in that bucket of water with the Colonel's feet in it. I do nothing but listen and nod, then salute and leave the tent. Lieutenant Anderson follows us out. Nobody says anything, there's nothing to say.

Anderson leads us to a waiting jeep with the engine warming. It's a first battalion jeep and the driver's in a hurry. He's probably been pulled out of some warm sack himself. He hardly even looks at us as we clamber into the back. Anderson hovers. He's wearing a side arm. He leans into the jeep. In the moonlight I can see him wink.

'Don't you guys do anything I wouldn't do.'

He steps back and the jeep lurches forward. It has chains for the mud and no lights. There's practically no road and the driver has his windshield folded down on the hood so he can see. Wilkins leans toward me, whispers.

'I guess that wink means we don't do anything, right, Will?'

But we *are* doing something already, driving in a jeep in the wrong direction in the middle of the night.

At the Third Battalion, a messenger from B Company is waiting for us. No more jeep. We start off behind him. He tells us to watch out for snipers and mortars. Snipers and mortars at midnight? We follow him to the Company Command Post. The farther forward we go, the dirtier, sloppier and more nervous the soldiers are. Twice we're challenged and need to give the password.

The Captain of B Company is expecting us. He briefs us again with another map. His map is folded and he pulls it out of his field jacket pocket. No celluloid. He's pale and nervous. He points out suspected emplacements. He has small Xs in pencil where there have been casualties. He pumps us for what we know. We tell him about the corps artillery at 0-five-thirty and the attack at 0-six hundred. He says there will be division artillery, as well as corps. He looks at his watch. He pulls one out of his field jacket pocket and gives it to Wilkins. Again, memories of D-3. He checks the time, winds it.

'You guys be out of there by 0-five hundred at the latest. We can't hold things up.'

He takes a good look at us. I'm embarrassed by our cleanliness. Compared to everybody around us we look like new replacements. This CP is in what used to be the cellar of a house. Rations, blankets, fartsacks, weapons are scattered around.

'Stay away from this wood right there. I'm pretty sure that's where they have at least an outpost. And if you see any tanks or personnel carriers or anything approaching the size of a squad, skedaddle on back here in a hurry.'

An even dirtier soldier comes through the blanket hung over the open cellar steps, he turns.

'Morris, take these two guys up to Brenner and Miodoser. Be careful, don't bring anything in on us. These guys are from Regimental I&R and are going out on a patrol.'

He smiles a thin smile and this Morris, who's a T5, looks at us as if we're from German headquarters. The Captain turns away and flops down on a cot with his muddy boots still on.

We go out into the dark. The moon is behind a cloud and we can't see much. We go about a hundred yards without saying anything. Morris scurries crouched over with his rifle at the ready. The moon comes out again. He hits the ground behind a pile of stones that might once have been a church. There's a part of a stone wall still standing, and something that could have been a stained glass window. He waves us forward and we slither up beside him. He whispers to us.

'Be careful, we could be under observation here, don't make any noise. I'll take you half way up to the outpost and then point out where you go.'

There's quavering fear in his voice.

We start crawling through the rubble. We're

ducking into every shadow from that moon. I mean, we're really crawling and fast, rifles out, swivelling along on elbows and hips. At least we're beginning to get dirty enough so we look as if we belong up here.

Morris keeps trying to explain how we can find the outpost ourselves, he's sure we can't miss it. He points to a small depression in the ground. We crawl out there without even knowing we've gone through the perimeter and are actually at a forward outpost. We slide on our stomachs the last seventy yards or so, until we get to the hole. Our guide has slithered on back. We creep up behind two more PFCs. These two are absolutely filthy, almost invisible in the mud. I give the password, just to be safe. They counter.

They tell us they're afraid even to go back through the area we've just come through. They're hungry, but not hungry enough to do that. They've been scraping the wax off K ration boxes and chewing on it. That gives us some idea of how ridiculous it all is, how scared and hungry these poor guys are.

By this time, we're fairly spooked ourselves; these guys have named every rock, tree, stump around them. They talk about the pointy rock out there and the lump of something on the ground at four o'clock, direction, not time. And they have seen, according to them, shadows moving a while ago that keep appearing and disappearing. It could only be the moon slipping in and out of the clouds, but I don't say anything. They've been sitting out here hours watching for things to move. It's one of those moonlit nights and everything is muddy, so in some places it shines and glistens, especially when there are puddles.

We're dirty ourselves after all the shimmying on our way out. There's a big difference between crawling and creeping, but no matter which you do, you have mud ground in your face and into every opening of your field jacket. When I'm flat on my belly shimmying along like that, I'm popping buttons off my field jacket, too. Wilkins finally asks the two of them.

'Which way should we go.'

There's a moment's silence. They look at each other.

'You guys have got to be nuts! You don't go *anywhere*; stay right here with us until somebody relieves us. We'll tell them how you went out.'

They're looking at us as if we're from that moon, with relatively clean uniforms, clean faces, and looking like people who've never been in a war at all. Compared to them, we're pristine, and they're filthy, absolutely stinking, like real bums. One rolls over on his back, takes out a cigarette, just sucks on it, doesn't light it.

'I'll tell you, there's no way anybody could get me to go out there. What's the good of it anyway?'

They won't even stick their heads up. They say things like, 'Look over there, see? Over there at one o'clock. You see that? We think there may be someone behind that rock, probably has a machine pistol.'

And they're not kidding, they're mostly scared.

So Wilkins and I decide to go out just a little way, see if there *is* actually anything.

We slither up and out of the hole carefully. The two left behind say they'll try covering us, but we're crazy. When we reach the first shady spot where we might be able to hide in the moon shadow, we both have the shakes. Wilkins stretches out on his back.

'You know Will, this is insane, we're going to get killed! Those people back there in their big comfortable tent at regiment don't care at all. They're only anxious to send us out and see how far we can go before somebody shoots at us.'

'Let's work our way over *there*.'

He points with the tip of his rifle to a blasted tree. 'We can tuck under that and figure this out.'

So we twist around on our stomachs again and start slithering in the mud until we're more or less out of breath. We wind up on our backs looking up at the sky. We lie out so my head is at his feet and his head is at my feet. That way, we cover all three hundred sixty degrees. We're talking to each other in low voices. We decide we can see what might be tank tracks, marks in the mud anyway. Also we aren't sure, but we hear motorised sounds. It could be our breathing, now we're scared silly.

We decide on this as our scenario: tanks, mostly because, in the hole, they told us they'd heard something that was either tanks or big trucks. To us, it's definitely tanks, now.

We also convince ourselves we see what looks like a three man mortar team just around another pile of rocks. We're scaring each other now. After fifteen minutes more of 'creative reconnaissance', we wriggle our way back to the outpost. They've been listening for the rat-tat-tat that would be the end of us.

They're really surprised to see us come back. We stay with them another fifteen minutes, telling them what we 'thought' we saw. We hang around a bit just to make it seem our patrol was longer than it really was, also to keep them company.

We snake our way back to the guy who took

us out here, then are taken back by the messenger of death through all the things we'd worked our way through the first time. We come to the jeep and now we're getting to feel like a couple of heroes returning from a dangerous mission. We have information on the enemy and are being escorted directly to the Colonel's tent at three o'clock in the morning, or whatever time it is by then. Wilkins forgot to give the watch back to the platoon leader, but it's so covered with mud we can't read it.

In the regimental tent, the Colonel's still all wrapped up in a blanket with his feet in a bucket of hot water, looking surprised as hell to see us. As far as he's concerned, it's like two dead men walking in through the flaps. We deliver our carefully rehearsed story of what happened and point out on the maps where we saw this. We really lay it on.

After that, the Colonel says we're brave boys, and he's going to put us in for bronze stars, but, of course, he never does.

In the attack the next morning, it turns out there's literally nothing out there for about three miles. The troops move ahead and nothing happens, no enemy action at all, the Krauts have pulled out. The Colonel gets a silver star for the advance, so he isn't about to take away his glory by giving us bronze stars. Of course we're convinced by now we deserve them, but we don't make a stink. That's the way it is in the army. We're not complaining too much, we're just glad to be alive.

In fact, Wilkins and I start worrying that they're going to find us out. What in heaven's name do they do to people who bring back false information? Hang them as traitors, torture them, fire them?

The strange thing is that after this attack, which goes on for almost four days, we mire down again in the mud, pure ineptitude and fear as far as we can figure. A kind of inertia sets in, everybody begins to see something behind every hill, bump or tree. Also, we have time to think. The Germans are doing the same thing too, probably.

We settle down and stay there for almost a week and this is just before we moved out to the Ardennes for some R&R, rest and recuperation.

We have some pretty bad things happen to the I&R around Metz because we have other patrols, one horrible one, in which we lose some of the Second Squad and Thompkins is killed. Four members on that patrol never come back.

We're pulled into reserve. We actually pull back

to our original lines. Somebody with a ruler must have drawn a nice straight line and decided to get rid of all the little bumps, including our forward one. We lose all the gain we made. All this scaredness, all this effort, all this everything, absolutely for nothing.

THE GALOSHES CAPER

It's near my nineteenth birthday now, and we're
near Metz. It's just continually raining. There's no
way to get dry, the big worry is trench foot. That
is, it's a worry for the few people out to win the
war. For us, getting trench foot and being sent back
to some hospital sounds like a special kind of
heaven. Guys start sleeping in their wet socks and
boots, hoping and praying. Trench foot looks as if
your toes have turned black and you have gangrene.
I guess, in a certain sense, that's what's happening.
We're hearing all the time about how at the hospital
they need to cut off toes or sometimes an entire
foot. Most of us consider losing a few toes a small
price to pay if we get to snuggle into a warm cosy
hospital bed, miles away from this insane scene,
and more importantly, have a chance to live.

But the officers find out about guys trying to get trench foot on purpose so they give lectures and demonstrations about not sleeping with boots on, taking our socks off, wringing them out, wearing them next to our chests to dry when we sleep and then changing them every day. But that won't stop trench foot, if all day long we're in mud with boots that absolutely soak up the water and just about every night we need to spend a minimum two hours on guard in a foxhole filled with water.

So, they bring up old time galoshes with clips on them that fit into slits and then are bent over. The trouble is they rattle. It's the kind of galoshes I used to wear to school in the winter as a kid. When we wear them they make more noise than a tambourine. Guys start throwing the galoshes away. They'd rather have trench foot than get shot. I can relate to that.

Next the word is sent out, that anyone who gets trench foot will be court-martialled and given a dishonourable discharge. Everybody's caught between a black foot and a hard place. But intentional trench foot goes on anyway.

Now I, personally, have a slight foot fetish. The calcaneus spur thing is quite enough. The idea of having black toes, or a foot cut off, is something

I can't live with. I'm trying to figure out a way to live and keep my toes. I come up with a crazy solution. I hunt around until I find a pair of galoshes somebody's thrown away, much bigger than I usually wear, about size fourteen. They're regular boats and a boat is just what I think I need. I try to dry out my own boots some, mostly by wiping them on my sopping blanket, then look around for someone with my boot size, eight and a half C, who's ready to trade four pair of reasonably dry socks for my boots. I convince this guy in L Company he can keep one pair of boots in the fartsack with him drying while he's wearing the other pair.

After I make the trade, I have eight pair of fairly dry socks. I put them on all at once and then slide my enlarged feet into my enlarged galoshes. I wiggle my toes around in there, then sleep with galoshes and socks in my fartsack tucked up against my stomach or between my legs. There's hardly enough room for the rest of me, but it works great. I make too much noise walking around, but my feet are comfortable. Every night I take off the galoshes and all the socks. The inner socks are generally dry. I sleep with all the socks tucked under my shirt. It works like a charm.

That is, it works like a charm until Sergeant

Ethridge notices how big my feet look. Under pressure, I explain. He says I'd better get my boots back or he's telling the Captain how I'm trying to get trench foot. What a moron. Three days later I slip the boots off one of the line company men who's dead. He's lying in the mud with a piece of shrapnel in his neck. The boots are size twelve D, almost like galoshes, and I wear them with all my socks. So, I escape Ethridge *and* trench foot. I'm pretty proud of myself until things get worse and a few toes missing doesn't sound so bad. Being in the infantry can certainly change one's priorities.

Another hard part about the mud is trying to keep the jeeps from getting stuck in it. We have chains on all the jeeps, but this mud is like thick glue, dark brown and deep. It's so deep that when we're trying to go over a hill off road in a field, one jeep pulling an equipment trailer gets stuck. We send another jeep to pull it out. This jeep gets stuck, too. Finally, we have six jeeps with two trailers stuck in that mud. Some of the chains need to be put on in the mud, another job for the I&R. We're all pushing, shoving and pulling, but the wheels keep spinning. The end is when the differential and axle sink into the mud. That's it. Also, my varicocele isn't happy. That doctor should be out here in the mud pushing and slipping with me.

In the end we need to contact a tank battalion in our sector to have them come over to pull the jeeps out. It's all very humiliating, as well as tiring. I wake up the next morning so stiff I can hardly move. It sounds like out of the frying pan into the fire, but we're all glad when the weather turns cold and the mud freezes. At least we can walk along reasonably well and there's no more trench foot. Also, the jeeps manage to buck their way over the frozen bumps.

MIKE HENNESSY

Not long after this, we go to relieve the Twenty-Eighth Division, The Yankee Division. They've just finished trying to charge up a hill on the old Maginot Line, now turned around to face the French. They had a really bad time, trying to retake the French forts in and around Metz. The Germans had turned the forts around against the French and improved the basically inept French design in many ways. One regiment of the Twenty-Eighth tried getting up the hill, which is, in reality, an underground fort. They slogged and crept through mine fields and past dug-in bunkers. It must have been frightening. Practically the whole regiment is wiped out. It's like the charge of the Light Brigade in some kind of a stupid old time war.

Most people in our outfit are not too happy

about charging up any hills. But I have a personal relationship with one member of this division.

When I was in elementary school, there was a young Irish boy named Mike Hennessy. He'd been left back a few times; he wasn't much of a student. That's putting it mildly, he was a Neanderthal. He had blue eyes, heavy black brows and black hair, he was somewhat stunted in growth, about the size all of us in the sixth grade were, when he should have been in the eighth. I was tenth, because I'd been double promoted once. He was fourteen and had to shave. The joy in his life seemed to be taking the joy out of my life. He was a real bully. I spent all of my recesses running around the school building trying to escape Mike Hennessy. One time he caught me, turned me upside down, pushed my head into the toilet and flushed it. I've never felt comfortable being in water since.

I hadn't thought much about Mike Hennessy in almost ten years. He left that school or I moved away, I don't know which. I didn't care too much as long as he was gone. They might have thrown him out of school, or he ran away; maybe they put him in reform school, he was always stealing things, letting air out of tyres, breaking windows, general mischief. He definitely needed reforming. But just by accident, while I was in Fort Jackson,

South Carolina, I met Mike Hennessy in the PX. He was easy for me to recognise. I'll never forget that brutal low-browed, long lipped, Irish face. He was in the Twenty-Eighth Division.

We shook hands, and here we are, both grown up, more or less, and he's two or three inches shorter than I am, and he actually even weighs less than I do. It doesn't seem possible. Even though the relationship of elementary school is gone, we could never be friends because he's as vulgar and stupid a man as he was a boy. He's almost drunk when I meet him, on three point two beer, yet. He's very definitely not the kind of person I can relate to. But we have a beer together for old times' sake. I realise he couldn't have been in a reform school or the army would never have drafted him, but he still looks like someone somebody ought to reform.

When we come up to relieve the Twenty-Eighth, on that steep hill near Metz, we all know what's happened and are scared. Luckily, someone has finally gotten smart, checked with the French and found how, for this particular fort, the one we're going to attack, Fort Drion, there are only two water sources, or wells. The sources fill great reservoirs dug inside the hill. These forts are really underground warrens. There's even an underground railway for moving guns and equipment. We find that out later. There are holes dug out in the sides of the hill to concrete bunkers. The sight of it is enough to scare anybody.

All of us in I&R are convinced they're going to send some of us up that hill to snoop around, find out where the bunkers are. We don't sleep much.

But the French tell us where the hidden springs are, so we poison them. Just like that. The glories of war. I don't know how, but somehow the Germans find out, maybe because people are dropping dead all around them and somebody guesses.

As soon as we arrive, the first thing I do is go see if Mike Hennessy has survived the 'Charge of the Light Brigade'. I go asking around the busy grave registrars on the Twenty-Eighth. Finally I find someone who knew him and is pretty sure he'd been hit. They've pulled most of the bodies down from the hill, I believe they even arrange a sort of truce for doing this.

Sure enough, there's Mike Hennessy stretched on the ground, his head sticking out of a body bag. It's a terrible shock to see someone who's been such a menace in your childhood, such a symbol of violence, unfairness and fear, who took so much of the joy away from your life, lying there empty, bloody, spattered with dirt particles and shrapnel pitted into his skin. He's white and blue, his whole shoulder blown off and his arm more or less tucked back in beside his body. The body bag is, in reality, a fartsack. He's still wearing his wool knit cap over his dark curly hair. One of his dog tags has been jammed in his mouth between his teeth. I'm not even nineteen years old yet, and Mike Hennessy is dead. Some things are hard to live past.

CAPTURE

Half of us are dug in on the hill, checking that the Germans don't come out of the fort. When they do sneak down, we shoot or capture them. Meanwhile, the other half of us are sleeping in a wooden barracks which had been the housing for the French soldiers when they manned the fort. It's a rather comfortable arrangement because there are bunks. Compared to what we've been having up till now, it's an incredibly safe, clean situation. We spend our time trying to scrape or wring the mud and water out of everything we own. We're all relaxed and enjoying ourselves; playing cards, shooting craps, reading, sleeping.

One night, I'm on guard at the barracks. It's only a two hour guard. We have six hours off and two on; very light duty. I'm leaning against a wall. There's a great grilled gate and I'm supposed to stop anyone from coming in. I've been told not to lean against the grille. I don't know why. The instructions are, I'm supposed to snap to and stand up with my rifle at 'ready' when any officer comes by; also keep anyone else without a special pass from going in. It feels something like toy soldiers, but I'm still shaking inside from Mike Hennessy.

I'm standing guard, half asleep, when someone taps me on the shoulder. I turn around and there's a German soldier with his hand out holding a canteen cup! I back off, unslinging my rifle from my shoulder. He seems unarmed and gets across to me by putting the canteen cup to his lips that all he wants is water. He's pale and his lips are dry and puckered. He's apparently snuck down from the fort somehow.

I push my rifle at him. He puts his hands on his head, still holding the canteen cup. I take him prisoner and start to bring him in. It turns out he has three buddies with him, they'd snuck down the hill, too, because they're dying of thirst. These guys join us and I march them back to the MPs. I give them all water from my canteen before handing them over. The next day the massive surrender occurs, and I keep thinking about how easily I could be as dead as Mike Hennessy. I had a canteen *full* of water hanging on my belt. That German soldier could have just killed me and taken the canteen, but he didn't.

FRANKLIN

After Metz, we have a new member come into the platoon. We need replacements and there's a constant changing of personnel as the normal death and wounded become more a part of our lives, and deaths. I'm getting more nervous all the time.

This replacement is quartered in my tent although he's already a T4, that is, the equivalent of a buck sergeant.

His name is Kurt Franklin and he's small, not more than five feet seven and wears glasses, not military metal rimmed glasses, but rimless. They make him look like a bank clerk or at least a company clerk. He has curly, short black hair. I can't figure why they put him in with me. Maybe they think I need some supervision after all the craziness with the forts, the gathering of the weapons, and most of all, the capture of all those prisoners. Also, I think they're beginning to catch on that I'm so scared.

The two of us are at about the same level of sloppiness, so as soldiers we don't get on each other's nerves. With us, it's sort of 'live and let live' as much as our situation has room for such an easygoing lifestyle.

My first impression is that he isn't just an ordinary soldier. For one thing, he's smarter and quieter. This is reinforced when they don't assign him to any particular squad position in the platoon. He isn't made Assistant Platoon Sergeant, either, although his rank would fit that job, and the assistant is in the hospital with measles.

He isn't assigned to any other company duties, either. And being assigned to Regimental Headquarters, with no duties, is about as close as one can get to being a civilian.

So, Kurt is a mystery to me and everyone else. I have a mystery tent mate. The whole squad keeps making guesses about who and what he is, but nobody comes up with anything.

We know he's called into the Regimental Headquarters tent often enough, even more than Anderson the I&R platoon leader. Twice, our main platoon rumour-monger, Miodoser, approaches Anderson and asks about Kurt, but Anderson only ignores him. How could anybody ignore Miodoser? He can be such a pest. So, after that, we leave well enough alone.

Then the first of the new two-man night patrols is assigned. It turns out I'm to go out with Franklin and try to find just where the German Regimental Headquarters has been established. It's not an I&R patrol, this is obviously a Tiger patrol, not our job. Somebody got mixed up. But, we go out just as it's getting dark. Kurt insists we leave in single file with me about a hundred yards behind him. This is not a normal patrol formation. Nothing is the way it should be. He waits till we're about two hundred yards out, going the *wrong* direction, as far as I'm concerned. I can hardly even see him, but I realise he's stopped after we've passed what was supposed to be the frontier outpost. He sits down beside a fallen tree and pulls a map out from under his shirt.

This, too, is something new. Sure, on patrols we sometimes have maps, but rarely do we actually take an official S2 generated map out with us. It's considered a serious security error. So, I sit with Kurt, sharing a security error beside a fallen tree.

He spreads the map out in front of us, holding down the corners with a few rocks. He looks over at me and smiles.

'Well, Will, what do you think of all this?'

What do I say to a question like that? I decide to just tell the truth.

'I think this might be the dumbest patrol I've ever been on and we could be killed any minute now just sitting here out in plain sight.'

He smiles again.

'You could be right. But I'll explain it all to you. You've been chosen as my special assistant in field interrogation. I work with the CIC, Civilian Interrogation Corps, and I'm really a First Lieutenant. You'll be getting a promotion to tech sergeant in a few days, but you're not to sew any stripes on or tell anybody until I give the word. Have you got that?'

I did not 'have' it and didn't want to, but he explains it all again and in detail.

'As you've probably guessed, we're coming to the end of this miserable war. There are many prisoners being taken all across the front. My family comes from Germany. I was born there and didn't leave until I was nine years old. In other words, I speak accentless German. My father and two little sisters didn't get out. I was brought out by my mother and grew up in New Jersey. We've never heard from the rest of my family. As far as we can tell, they were probably killed by the Nazis, and just because my father was Jewish.'

He reaches up and carefully pulls off his fragile glasses. He wipes them on a flannel handkerchief he keeps in a little leather case. I've seen him do this before. He slides them back on, hooking them behind one ear after the other. He stares at me some more, tears in his eyes.

'I'm one American soldier with something to fight about. But, I admit I'd like to kill at least five German men for every one of my family they've killed.'

He pauses. He has me scared. I don't need anything like this. Up until now, there's been nothing personal for me in this war; just killing the enemy, the Krauts.

'Don't tell anybody I've told you this. If one of the Division staff officers finds out about how I feel, they'd probably pull me off this CIC detail. I'm counting on you.'

Why the hell is everybody counting on me? This war doesn't mean anything to me except it'll probably kill me. I'm liable to be dead, all over nothing. I don't say anything. I figure this Kurt for some kind of maniac. I'm *not* a maniac, I'm scared out of my wits, yes, but I don't really want to actually kill anybody. I nod my head, the way you would with any crazy, and don't say anything. This Kurt Franklin is a dangerous man. Hell, Franklin isn't even a Jewish name, I don't think.

I wait. Then I can't wait any more.

'So, what are we doing out on this patrol? Are you going to find and kill the whole German high command or something? This all seems nuts to me.'

'Don't worry, Will. I just wanted to see how you'd react. There's a lot of anti-Semitism all through the American army. Most of these guys I just can't trust. If they were Germans they'd probably be killing Jews themselves. It's all crazy.'

'So, again, what are we doing out here sitting in a field waiting to be killed? Let's go back.'

'We're safe here. I've checked. I needed to find a place where I could talk to you in private. Can I trust you?'

'You'd better trust me. If what you're saying is true, we're probably breaking at least ten of the Articles of War. Who's the enemy? Which direction are they? Do we start killing American non-coms? Are we going to arrange for another of those group surrenders the way we did in Metz? I don't get it.'

'It's like this, Will, simple enough. There will be more and more Krauts coming in to surrender, some of them will be their officers, some staff or intelligence officers, many of them SS, or former Hitler Youth. It's the Twelfth Panzer out in front of us now, an SS elite command. These officers will be funnelled on back to your S2. He works with the CIC, too, and speaks some German he learned at Yale. He's supposed to interrogate these guys.'

'So?'

'We're convinced they have information about troop emplacement, planned attacks, names and sizes of Kraut forces out there that would help us a lot, maybe avoid some unnecessary killing.'

'So, what's that got to do with me? I don't speak German, I almost failed Latin in high school. What makes you think I can make them tell me anything? I thought you wanted to kill all these Krauts anyway.'

'You are a smart ass, aren't you? I've been told you don't have much respect for non-coms or officers, but this is different.'

'In the army, everything is always different, if it isn't the army way. So what else is new?'

'Don't be difficult, Will. When we interrogate these guys it will always be in the field. They'll already have had their chance to spill their guts back at S2 interrogation centres or here at your I&R headquarters. They'll only send the "hard core cases" out to us.'

'Sounds like Mafia business to me. I imagine the Red Cross or MPs could make quite a case out of this.'

'Don't worry about the MPs or the Red Cross. That's all being taken care of. These guys won't be speaking any more English than you speak German. I'll be doing all the interrogation. You'll just be backing me up.'

'You mean, with an M1 or one of the new "grease guns"? That should be fun!'

'You don't shoot anybody, just act tough and push them around some. Remember, these guys have been killing people as if it's going out of style. These are real gangsters, garbage, a menace to the human race.'

'You don't need to convince me. I went to all the propaganda movies, John Wayne, Van Johnson, Alan Ladd are the good guy heroes and Lew Ayres the yellow coward. My questions is still "Why me?" You tell me I'm going to make "tech" for doing nothing more than I'm doing now, right?'

Franklin takes off his helmet, wipes his brow with the back of his hand. It's the first time I realise how serious he is about all this. I'm listening, but the entire thing seems so bizarre, out of some other crappy movie.

'It's because you were so effective with that capture in Metz to start things off. I went through records of about fifty guys, photos and all, making decisions. I'm down to five guys in your division. I'll choose three from these. You'll never know who the others are unless we work together on a project, except they're generally in I&R, they'll never know about you.'

'You still haven't answered my question.'

'Don't laugh. It's because of the way you look! The Germans all have this goofy conviction of how a good, meaning "bad" German should be taller than most, with blue eyes and blond hair, the true Nordic type. You're perfect! You almost scare a little Jew like me.'

'Cut it out!' Sure, I used to be called 'Whitey' as a kid because my hair would bleach out in the sun, and some of the dumb girls in class would start on how blue my eyes were, but that's all. I've never won any beauty contests. I'll admit maybe I was a good looking baby. But that's never meant anything to the army.

'You've won the Infantry Baby Beauty Contest and the prize could be your life. Think about that!'

He stands up and I stand up, too. We start back the way we came. When we reach the perimeter, he turns to me.

'Well, what do you say, Will?'

'When do they start the "tech" pay? And I already have some salary deductions I've lost the hard way. Do they wipe those off my service record?'

'That's already been done.'

'Pretty sure of yourselves aren't you?'

'More sure of you, Will. We'll be seeing each other. Remember, not a word to anybody. Not even Anderson knows about this. I'll be transferred out of your squad tomorrow. If anybody asks, we didn't find anything out there. There actually isn't much according to the aerial surveys.'

With this he continues to walk away from me and I turn to where my tent is. I'll have it to myself for a while.

During most of the months of March and April I'm called regularly to help with 'Interrogation'. For a while, they actually put me up in one of the regimental tents. When I'm not being a terrorist, I'm living high.

Kurt is right. The guys they throw to us are blond, blue-eyed giants all right, perfect Nazi movie types. And they *are* arrogant. Their uniforms are fairly clean with polished boots, but one can see from their faces, and the way they move, that they've had some recent rough treatment. Kurt scares me when he goes into his act. He scares them, too. He's usually pushing his face into theirs or actually into their necks and jamming a pistol or 'grease gun' into their stomachs and hollering at them.

The Germans are pretty impressive the way they resist. Mostly we have some Poles who've attached themselves to our outfit who punch them around. At the time, I didn't realise they had good reason.

They'd get them down on the ground and use their boots to grind their faces into the mud or snow. Then they kick them, not seeming to care where they kick. And these Germans are so damned nasty and tough, one can't help rooting for the Poles.

Finally, we have a pair of young SS officers. They look to be about the age of our Lieutenant. Kurt tells us that they're both from an Intelligence Company something like Sicherheitsdienst and *these* guys we've got to 'break'.

The Poles don't get anything out of them with the rough stuff. Then Kurt tosses out shovels to them and shouts. He wants the Germans to lie down on the ground. With a bayonet he marks off spaces on the ground for the two of them, just large enough to match their bodies. It makes me think of two things from childhood. The times we'd bury each other at the beach in the sand, and the times we'd do the same thing in winter to make angels in the snow.

Kurt gets them digging. It's a grey, cold day. They start working up a sweat and Kurt is hollering at them the whole way. I can't understand what he's saying, but I can understand when he starts shooting at their feet and between their legs. He actually nips one of them on the boot. He's shooting from the hip all the time and can't have that much control.

Every once in a while he has them stretch out in the holes they're digging. Their faces are turning whiter than the snow. I'm tempted to just walk away. This is more than I bargained for. I feel like a Nazi myself.

When the holes are dug, Kurt has them strip off all their clothes, including underwear, then stretch out in the holes. Now they've started shouting back and crying. When one seems to have gone too far with his curses and anti-Semitic raging, Kurt pulls off a few shots near his head. I don't know how he can miss. Either he's a very good shot or a poor one. It doesn't matter much in terms of the effect on these poor bastards.

When he has the two of them stretched out on the cold, dark ground and white muddied snow, he has the Poles begin to bury them. He's giving instructions all the time in an almost hysterical voice. He has them start at their feet and work their way up toward the heads until only their faces are showing out of the slush. He's asking the same questions all the time. Obviously asking if they'll talk to the interrogators. One of them breaks down as they start sprinkling the earth on his face. Kurt gives the word and two of the Poles drag his almost unconscious body out of his grave. He's slobbering and vomiting as he's dragged off to the regimental interrogation tent.

It doesn't take long until the second officer gives in too. A human mind can only take so much. When the Poles lift him up, he breaks away and starts running with his numb legs. Kurt lets him go about twenty yards, running and stumbling, then shoots him in one of his legs just at the knee. He falls screaming and rolling.

That's the last I see of it. We're in a daze. I think Kurt suffers almost as much as the Germans. The Poles, on their own, are filling in the holes. Maybe in some way it helps them to forget what has just happened. But I know I can never forget. That's the end of my career on the interrogation detail.

I go back and sleep two days in my tent, chasing away the nightmares.

SERGEANT ETHRIDGE

During the course of the war, I change. It's probably just inborn cowardice. Not through any great effort or skill on my part, I find I'm scared more than most people. And, I'm not adept at hiding how scared I am from the other guys. I'm definitely not known by our squad as the most courageous of soldiers, despite taking prisoners at Metz. I'm not so bad that they're actually thinking of throwing me out of the I&R, that is sending me back to a line company, something we all dread, but it's bad enough. I discover the difference between being scared and being a coward is having other people find out.

I become quite a specialist at what we call 'dogging it', that is, faking a patrol the way Wilkins and I did. We all do it. If the situation looks really bad, we become quite imaginative mocking up our phoney, *ersatz* war. Also, we get good at ducking, hiding out, when a dangerous patrol is being formed.

Once, when I know before anyone else that there is going to be the worst kind of patrol, 'Tiger', where we're supposed to take a prisoner, I hunker down under a jeep. I'm not too proud of this.

A Sergeant named Ezra Ethridge is in charge of the I&R platoon. I know he's looking for me. I'm falling asleep under that jeep, trying not to breathe. Ethridge is another southern cracker, a real regular army non-com, and we all hate him with a passion.

Ethridge doesn't like anybody, but it seems he particularly loathes me. Maybe it's the way I goof off all the time. Anyway, he's always taking it out on me. And so I know tonight's patrol is going to be really nasty.

A good friend of mine named Vance Watson is now my tent buddy, when and if we ever have a tent. Mostly we're in holes. The main reason we get along is because it's a contest between us who's the most scared. We just *know* we're scheduled for this patrol. We'd heard news of it, it's definitely the kind of thing we don't want to do.

We've found an old barn near the Headquarters CP in which someone must have stored hay. It's our secret, last ditch, hideout. We go up there on a sort of shelf and pile hay over each other and become invisible whenever things look bad. When no one is looking, I make a surreptitious dash out from under the jeep and head for our hideout. Vance is already there.

Ten minutes after our dash we're settled in. It's about twenty-two hundred, past ten o'clock. We're pulling our wool knit caps over our ears, trying not to hear Ethridge yelling, resting our heads on our helmets turned upside down. We also know that even if we aren't on this patrol and they find us, we'll be assigned to some other ratshit duty, like helping the officers bunk in, carrying all their crap.

Ethridge is hollering all over the place. Now, I have to say, this is the kind of thing you can really feel bad about, *but not us*. We're just ducking down deeper and deeper, thinking he'll never find us, he'll never climb that rickety ladder, he's too fat, he'll break it.

He never does find us for that patrol and he sends out two other guys from the Second Squad, one named Jim Freise and the other Al Toby. It's a bad patrol, as bad as we thought, or even worse.

But thank God neither of them is killed. Jim takes a bullet right through his thigh, but it doesn't break his thigh bone. Al Toby carries Jim all the way back, three hundred yards. Luckily Toby is about six-two and strong as an ox, Jim Freise maybe five-eight and light. Jim Freise looks a bit like Mike Hennessy, the same kind of dark curly hair and blue eyes. After Toby brings Jim in and slides him off his back, he falls in a heap on the ground. Medics carry Jim off on a stretcher, unconscious, medics hovering over him.

Of course, Vance and I feel like real rotters. I actually find myself wishing I'd gone, the war would be over for me. Jim got one of those million dollar wounds, one where he'll never be in combat again.

Ethridge gives us a bad time about how someone else took our patrol and was practically killed, all that kind of crap. Where the hell were we? Couldn't we hear him calling? But Sergeant Ezra Ethridge never once went on a patrol himself. He knew it and we knew it.

CROSSFIRE

Despite all these kinds of dumb patrols and because three of our non-coms are killed by some eighty-eight millimetre direct hits, I do become squad leader to the first squad of the I&R platoon. I can't believe it, attrition can do wonders.

The war seems as if it's never going to end. We're deeper into Germany. We go several days when there'll be practically no fighting, no serious resistance, and then we get stopped, mostly by artillery. Unfortunately, we're involved with pene-trating the Siegfried Line, now, the Germans' major defensive line, their equivalent to the French Maginot Line, only much more intelligently designed. They've rearranged it so their bunkers are in groups of three, in triangles, each one covering the other two. After a lot of trial and error, i.e. casualties and deaths, we all sort of figure it out. You don't go for either of the front bunkers; you go for the back one, the third one. Then, when you've cut that third one out you've broken down their system of mutual defence and you can come up behind the other two bunkers. Then, if they don't surrender, we drop or throw grenades through the firing ports.

Sometimes it takes twenty grenades to get one in. It's like a carnival game. But after a while, a Kraut usually pushes out a white flag and surrenders. By this time, the Germans have passed the word around that if the back bunker is taken '*alles ist kaput*', they'd better surrender or shrapnel will be ricocheting around them in the bunker.

None of this kind of thing is really I&R work but things are thoroughly screwed up; military term, SNAFU. We're doing almost everything from attack patrols to guarding the regimental band.

We're in snow now, it has to be late January, somewhere in there. As usual, we don't know what the situation is. One afternoon they call me in, as squad leader. There's Sergeant Ezra Ethridge, along with the new S2, Major Woods, who had been in charge of the motor pool before. The rumour is that Love, our former S2, went bonkers with combat fatigue. That I can understand. There's also Lieutenant Anderson, our platoon Lieutenant who never goes on patrol either, who knows next to nothing about combat.

This S2, Major Woods, whose experience has been just keeping trucks and jeeps running, has come up with a really dumb patrol. Patrolling is none of his business, and this one is absolutely impossible. It's as if I went down and rebuilt one of the jeep engines.

We're in the ruins of a town called Olsheim. There's nothing but bare, deep, snow fields in front of us, there's hardly a tree or a bush. The Major has spread out some old aerial photographs on a rickety table, which indicate there's either a railway embankment or a bunker out there in front of us but it's hidden in the snow. I look at it and even though I know I should keep my mouth shut, I can't help blurting out, 'This looks like big trouble to me, Sir. This is something for a real "Tiger" patrol, not I&R.'

Anderson is agreeing with me. He thinks this is not an I&R patrol situation at all, it should be a 'Tiger' patrol with twenty or thirty 'line' soldiers and artillery backup.

I speak up again: 'You can't just send a reconnaissance patrol out on this kind of mission, Sir;

it's suicide. Reconnaissance is only supposed to find out what things look like, and come back. If anybody comes close enough to see what's actually going on out here, for sure they aren't coming back.'

But I'm low man on the totem pole at this conference, nobody's paying any attention to my ranting and raving. Finally, after I give my little speech about how it's impossible, and Lieutenant Anderson gives his, Sergeant Ethridge comes on heavy.

'This *is* what I&R is supposed to do, Wharton. It's intelligence reconnaissance. You can't just sit back here on your fat asses and play at being intelligent, you've got to go out and reconnoitre.'

'Wharton, you're to take out this patrol and I want the whole Second Squad to go with you. I don't want to hear another word. Just do some reconnaissance work for a change and check this out. That's your job.'

Major Woods, who's been starting to back off on the idea of the patrol himself, is now effusive with his enthusiasm and 'go get 'em' mentality.

What can I do? I mean, I know what I should do. I should refuse to take out the patrol. I should just say no.

But I don't.

After the meeting, I try talking to Ethridge and

he accuses me of being yellow. That's true, but it's not for him to say. He's never even been out on a patrol. I go back to the squad and tell them what's happened. These are all bright guys. They figure it out fast. They're a little pissed off at me for not protecting them, but they're willing to do it.

'Look,' I say quietly to them when we're all together, 'we're going to put on snowsuits and whiten our rifles. We're going out to where they can't see us from here, not even at the outposts. Then we're going to flop in the snow. We'll be cold, but we're going to stay out for maybe an hour, and stay alive. Then we'll come trooping back in and say we didn't see anything.'

I pause. No one speaks. I go on.

'If tomorrow some other outfit is stupid enough to go out there and they run into trouble, we're sorry, but it is not an I&R patrol.'

There isn't much argument. Nobody's happy but we agree. We prepare ourselves as best we can. It's a scary patrol, just going out there, no matter what. We need to go a long way from where we are here, visible all the way, until we're out of sight of the perimeter guard, and of the regular dog soldiers on line out there. It's the only way. We need somehow to be invisible but we'll be visible as hell. I mean it's not a full moonlight night but there's *some* moonlight, enough so when you stand you cast a shadow. White casts a dark shadow on white no matter how you do it. You think you're invisible but you're not.

So we take off around midnight or so, assuming Jerry will have minimum guard out, that is, if there's anyone there at all, and if there's going to be trouble. The problem is we don't actually know what to expect; we're going out blind.

Right at the ridge line, above this long open uphill plain of snow, is a pine forest. It worries me, anything could be in there, even tanks. Just in front of the trees is where these questionable lumps covered with snow are located. But, when one is out there in the snow it's hard to figure what they are.

We go in standard patrol formation, at five yard intervals with two scouts out. I'm the third one in line, just behind the scouts. Then the rest of the squad is behind me, followed by the assistant squad leader, Russ. We're trooping along through the snow; it's deep enough to get in our galoshes. I'm looking back constantly, more than anyone else, trying to estimate the distances. Just how visible are we, from behind, as well as from in front? Now we're out in the deep snow we're practically snow blind, and there's a light ground fog. It's hard to figure just how far we've come. When is it they won't be able to see us from the outposts? In my mind, the real enemy, as far as we're concerned, is behind us. We slog on out there in the open snow and I give the signal to hit the ground, that is, the snow. Then I turn around, on my knees. I have a pair of binoculars on me which I'm not supposed to have. Binoculars are for officers. I took this pair from a dead German officer.

I look back and can still see the guys back in the foxholes on the perimeter. We're not far enough out yet. I look forward and can't see anything; no way I can figure out what those lumps are either. I whisper back along the line:

'I think we'll go another hundred yards, then we'll have guaranteed we did it, they won't be able to see where our footsteps end in daylight, with everybody charging out on the attack. Because they'll be attacking at dawn, they'll trample down our footsteps without seeing them.'

I guess there's a good psychological reason for armies always attacking at dawn. They say it catches the enemy when he's least expecting it, theoretically. But, you're also sending out your own troops at their least vital time. Why do humans, especially military humans, like to do things the hard way? I'm not saying war can be fun, but it doesn't have to be so hard.

So we scramble up again, wiping the snow off. We're moving forward and can see a lump looming up slightly to our right. It's one I hadn't seen at all before. It looks just like a railroad overpass, but I don't see any railroad tracks. I'm thoroughly confused. So we hit the ground fast and stay there. Nothing happens.

I whisper to one of the two scouts, Richards.

'I'm going up to go look into this one, I don't think there's really anything there; but if we go and look in we can at least back up our story.'

Richards stands up.

'Sure, that's okay with me. I'll go with you and give you cover.'

When we get up close, he volunteers to check this bump out himself. Somewhere about here, I should have called the whole thing off. We didn't really need to know what was under that questionable railroad overpass.

But no, I stretch out in the snow with my rifle to cover him. He goes forward and round a corner of snow and disappears into a hole.

The next thing I know, he comes tearing out of there, running like hell. Behind him is rifle fire and he hits the ground trying to get his rifle up. It looks as if half the German army comes storming on out after him.

I start firing madly, fifteen rounds from my carbine, then I'm trying to switch the clip. Here we are, this is *real* war, shooting at each other like cowboys and Indians. Then the Germans see there are others behind me and dash back into their hole. I don't know how it happens, but they must have a phone there.

What we thought might be a railroad overpass is a bunker, and is one of a set. There are two others up higher. This one has its back turned to protect the other bunkers. We've walked straight into a trap.

The whole squad is smack in the middle of an open snow covered field, the forest line is up the hill ahead of us. From its edge now starts machine gun fire, crossfire, covering where the whole squad is spread out. They're shouting, shooting, screaming, hollering, running, falling, trying to get away but they're all caught in this devastating crossfire. Nothing has happened to me yet, but both the scouts are down. The assistant squad leader, Russ, was shot down right away and Cochran, the one who was supposed to supply covering fire for me, is down too, I see him thrashing in the snow.

Instead of an M1 rifle he had a carbine. He'd filed down the sear like mine, making it automatic. So he had fifteen shots. That seems like a lot of fire power, but it's not enough. It should also be the perfect weapon for this short distance, but it's not enough.

I look back and see most of the squad being mowed down. Some are running and some are trying to hunker down and return fire, but it's hopeless. I figure there's no way I can stay here, and no way I can surrender. These people aren't interested in me surrendering.

I figure if I can just run fast enough *up* the hill I can maybe get between the lines of fire of those machine guns. I can tell already that they're just sweeping back and forth, they're not hand-held guns, they're mounted, and therefore have a particular limited traverse. If I can get into the cone between where they reach, I'll have half a chance. This all runs through my mind in seconds. I take off faster than I can think. I jump back and forth expecting every second to have my head blown off or feel my legs go out from under me.

Somehow, by a miracle, I get between the bunkers and above the crossfire. I work my way into the forest. I look downhill and nobody's moving, none of us, and no Germans. I keep looking, but I don't think there's anyone to see, anyone alive, that is.

This is a strong point we've run into not a defensive line. It's one strong point in their system of defence. When they're in retreat they set these up to defend their rear. Usually they have telephone connection with the main body of troops to let them know when someone attacks. For us it's the worst it could have been, we definitely walked right into it blind.

I do, luckily, break out so I'm behind the field of fire of those two machine guns. I stretch out to get my breath and up chuck. I don't know what else is hidden in this forest. Slowly, I work my way sideways, then, later, carefully back through the perimeter of another company down the line. I'm lucky I don't get myself killed by them. I'm hollering and screaming, 'American, I'm American, don't shoot, don't shoot.' D-3 all over again.

I come with my hands up, my carbine dangling on my shoulder, up to their foxhole. Two GIs I've never seen are in it, I drop like a dead man, trembling all over, feeling horribly guilty about everything, at the same time, scared to death. These GIs let me rest a little, then lead me back to a kitchen tent. From there, at about 0-six hundred, I'm worked back to where I'm supposed to be, at

Headquarters Company. The corps artillery has started like thunder in a fish bowl.

By this time I've gotten some of my strength and morale back, also about fifty per cent of my reason, at the most. I'm mad-angry as well as scared. My guilt had transformed itself into pure, unadulterated, murderous anger. I'm insane with it. I know Ethridge is bunking in one of those A tents with the motor pool guys. It's farther back than it's supposed to be. I'm convinced he's a physical coward, even worse than I am.

I should have known he'd be way back there. He digs himself a foxhole, or has it dug for him, every time we set up camp. I don't blame him. We've recognised each other, it's a mutuality which is not respect.

I go in the tent and find the cot with Ethridge in it, sleeping on his back, big belly out, wearing his GI underwear, three blankets, more than any of us have. I'm amazed he isn't in his hole. These are the things I note in passing. I still have my rifle with me. I stand over his bed and yell, curse him. As he wakes, staring, I jam the butt of my rifle down hard in the centre of his fat stomach. I don't shoot him, you've got to give me credit. I want to, but I don't. It turns out later this blow cracked the bottom of his sternum and broke four ribs on one side. I had no idea I'd hit him that hard. But it did wake him up. I got his attention.

He slides off his cot, groaning, stands. I swing my rifle and smack him in the face. His face turns red with blood, he's screaming. I'm out of control. I'm yelling about what a yellow assed coward he is, and tell him how the whole squad is dead out there in the snow because of him. I'm so worked up, I can hardly talk. I can't breathe. Three motor pool guys roll out of their cots. One has some kind of heavy duty flashlight they use for repairs on the jeeps. He hits me with it then shines it in my eyes. They see Ethridge standing there, rocking back and forth, crying and cursing, frothing blood. They jump me and throw me on the ground. I don't even struggle. I don't have the strength left. I can only cry.

Ethridge is such a mess they call in the medics. They converge and I'm pulled back, my rifle's taken.

They don't want to wake the Company Commander yet. They take turns standing guard over me in an empty pup tent. When Anderson comes, he's in shock and begins reading the riot act to me.

'What the hell happened?'

I just sit there.

'Where's the rest of the squad?'

I look up at him, at his clean, white face.

'Dead, they're all dead Lieutenant, thanks to you and Ethridge.'

It turns out I'm wrong. One other guy, one of the new rifleman replacements, did the same thing I did, following me instinctively. I'm the squad leader, so he's just following me.

Somehow he worked his way back up into the woods. He comes in afterward through C Company. The rest of the squad is still out there, all dead, no one moving. They find them all the next day. I don't go out to look. I'm confined to quarters.

COURT MARTIAL

The next day I'm called in front of Colonel Douglas Moore, our Regimental Commander. The S2, Lieutenant Anderson, and the PFC who escaped with me, are there. I tell what we'd come on and how fast it all happened. After the Colonel goes through a lot of nonsense about abandoning my men, I tell how I think it was all Sergeant Ethridge's fault. He's the one who insisted on the patrol although both Lieutenant Anderson and I tried to point out the danger involved. Major Wood didn't know enough to know how dangerous and stupid it all was. It just wasn't the kind of patrol an I&R platoon does. Lieutenant Anderson backs me up. Neither of us really badmouths the new S2 major, Major Wood. It'd only make things worse.

Things are quiet. The Colonel looks us over seriously. In my mind, I can still see him that night wrapped in a shawl, his feet in a bucket of hot water.

'Soldier, this warrants a special or general court martial, you all know that. Sergeant Ethridge can never serve in the army again. He doesn't have enough teeth. I've recommended him for an honorable discharge, a purple heart and a bronze star. He'll receive a full pension as a disabled veteran.'

He pauses.

'And you, Sergeant Wharton, due to extenuating circumstances, this is only a summary court martial. It will not be marked against you in your service record except as that. However, you are hereby broken in rank to buck private and transferred out of Headquarters Company back to K Company in the Third Battalion. I don't want to hear any more about this disgraceful incident.'

He pauses to see I've got the message.

'At ease,' he says, then continues: 'Off the record, do you realise what you've done, Wharton, attacking a superior non-commissioned officer? You almost killed him. I just got back the medical report from the field hospital. His military career is definitely over. Maybe you did him a favour. Frankly, he'd gotten to the point where he wasn't

174

doing his job, he was scared all the time and taking it out on the men. I would have had to replace him.'

'As for you, Wharton, I'm going to try keeping this a summary court martial and see if we can get by with it. I don't think Major Wood is going to make anything of this because he doesn't want it known how he set up this patrol under these conditions.'

Now this regular army bird colonel, Colonel Moore, has control over not just the I&R. He has an entire band within Regimental Headquarters. There are a whole raft of people, the cooks, the laundry and the motor pool people, who really don't have much to do with war. They just keep things going. They're headquarters' personnel. The I&R is the only part of a headquarters company which usually has anything to do with actual fighting and even we, most of the time, rarely do. Ours is a soft berth compared to a line company, except when we need to go on these nutty patrols. So, I'm not enthusiastic about going up to a line company.

That day I'm broken back to private. I clear my things from the company kitchen truck and ship out of the Intelligence and Reconnaissance platoon back to my original company, K Company.

There have been considerable recent losses in K

Company so I'm put in as a replacement. It's a dangerous situation to be in. As a new replacement I'll get all the toughest jobs, but I'm happy to get off with my skin, even if it's only temporary. To be honest, I was really hoping they'd go all the way, send me back and put me in prison. Anything to get out of combat. Lucky Ethridge.

However, at the same time, I'm worried about being stuck with a dishonourable discharge and a whole mess of terrible things I've been conditioned to fear. Even though I know war is a dumb thing, I don't want to come out of it with the lifelong stigma of a dishonourable discharge.

I recognise now that the only heroes of wars are the conscientious objectors. But all the junk they'd pumped into my eighteen year old mind was against me. I didn't have enough information and, also, I probably didn't have enough courage.

As soon as I'm packed I get driven, over muddy roads, by the Headquarters Company cook. He'd been a friend of Ethridge, so he sees me as the villain and won't speak to me the whole way. I know the entire motor pool is against me. They'd won a lot of money from Ethridge playing poker and I've almost killed the golden goose.

When I get to K Company, after I've checked in with the Company Commander, I hunt around to find my old K Company friends, but most of them are gone, killed or wounded. They've been continuously on the attack since the time I left them, and it stays that way.

CHAMPAGNE PARTY

Because I'd been a sergeant and an old member of the company, the Commander of K Company, Captain Wall, kind of takes me under his wing. He moves me up pretty fast. Not as fast as they moved Sergeant Hunt, the trigamist, but fast enough. I find out Captain Wall is the fifth K Company Commander, the other four were killed. And Captain Wall looks as if he might have already been killed and doesn't know it.

That bad patrol I took out and lost left me on the edge of sanity, if there'd been any left. I can't work at anything consistently. I just spend my time constantly thinking, 'How can I get out of this, how can I manage to stay alive and not kill any more people?'

In March, I'm saved from going psycho by being

wounded. It's a minor wound, a piece of shrapnel in my wrist and another lodged in my groin, but the fascinating thing is after they've repaired the shrapnel wounds, I spend my time wandering all around the hospital having a hard time standing up.

At night, I can't even make it to the john in the dark, and no one knows what's wrong. I buy a flashlight for nights. I think I might finally be going psycho but they think I'm goofing off. It turns out that in the powerful one hundred and fifty five mm explosion of an American artillery shell right next to me, the one that gave me the shrapnel wounds, I seem to have lost the vestibular and semicircular canals in my ears. I don't know this yet, and the doctors don't either. Also, the repair they did in my groin at the field hospital, taking out some shrapnel and stitching the muscles together, didn't work right. I need to have it redone later.

However, it's slowly coming toward the end of the war. For reasons I still don't understand, when we cross the Rhine, they round up all the walking wounded, including me. I'm considered walking, although wobbly. I walk rather peculiarly because if you don't have any vestibular canals you don't have much in the way of balance. I'm walking around like a drunken sailor, complaining of being dizzy all the time, not knowing what the matter is, and everybody's telling me the American one five five shells went off to close to me and my brains were shaken up a bit but it will be all right. I'm something like a punch drunk fighter.

Everything now is rough and ready. The doctors are suspecting everyone of trying to get out of combat for medical reasons. They are. However, at the same time, I have something seriously wrong and they won't listen. It's a bit like 'cry wolf'; when it comes to the real thing, they won't believe me. They send me back to my outfit, to K Company. We cross the Rhine River in little boats with the help, of all things, of the US Navy. American troops have already crossed the river up north of us, over the Remagen railroad bridge, so this crossing is totally unnecessary. It's probably because they've got all this equipment ready to do a water crossing; they're going to do it anyway, practising for the next war maybe, who knows. Anyway, we bounce across, and I'm miserable. I can hardly hold a rifle, one arm is completely bandaged and I have a sling. I don't need to keep my arm in the sling, so I have it slung around my neck, sort of for decoration and maybe to ring up a note of pity. I'm like something out of a French Revolutionary War painting by Delacroix.

We get on the other side and charge up the slippery slope of the Rhine River bank. We have had little trouble crossing, no heavy fire at us or anything, just some random small arms stuff. Probably civilians defending their home turf from the marauding Americans. The Germans know we crossed at Remagen, a bridge someone forgot to blow up, and so they've generally pulled back. They're just a bit smarter than our officers. It's a challenge, climbing and scrambling through grape-vines on the steep bank, but we finally get to the town of Koblenz.

Well, there are enough German soldiers left in the town to make it tough. It's the only street fighting, house to house, operation I'm involved in during the entire war. We're going along, block by block, trying to capture and hold high points, flushing out snipers. We'd think we have them all, when some other fanatic would start picking us off. Usually three or four GIs will be down before we can figure out where the sniper is. Then we'll toss a grenade, or lob in some mortars, whatever it takes.

I decide to retire from this war for a little while. The whole affair's getting to be like something straight out of a grade C movie and I don't want to be involved. I duck down in a cellar and hang out there until I stop hearing rifle fire, grenade bangs and mortar thumps.

I don't think any prisoners are taken and I don't care much. In the wine cellar where I'm hiding, I discover racks and racks of champagne! This isn't champagne country, so it must be stuff the Germans confiscated in France. I'm down there and I don't know how to open a champagne bottle, especially with my hand still bandaged. The wire wrappings are hard to get off.

Finally, I get the wire off, and it pops, so I lose most of the champagne because it isn't cold enough. I've never been a big drinker, but I'm dying of thirst because there isn't any water, so I drink champagne.

When everything has settled down and the guys come back, I tell them what I've found. I should have known better. They come charging down to my cellar. Everybody takes a bottle, figures out how to open it and we're all down there drinking champagne, bubbles flowing out our mouths and over everything.

Then someone has the idea it would be fun to take a champagne bath like one of those naked movie stars. We're all filthy and sweaty anyway. We form long lines like a fireman's bucket brigade and pass the bottles up two floors to the bathtub.

We fill the bathtub with this bubbly wine. Unfortunately, the guys at the tub don't know the first thing about how to get the corks out either, so they're just knocking the necks against the wall and pouring what's left into the tub. It's a real bash, like the celebration of a winning team after a football game. We take turns in the tub. As soon as the champagne gets so we can't see the bottom of the tub we pull the plug, let it drain out, and start the bucket brigade coming up from the cellar again.

Then, of course, we can't find anything to dry ourselves with and we're all sticky. It's something we didn't think of. So, we rip down the drapes in this handsome house. The windows are about two storeys high. We dry ourselves off on the drapes and then dress again. Our pants, even our underwear, are sticking to us. And we're still drinking champagne. People are passing out dead drunk or throwing up all over the place. The last thing I remember is standing in a doorway, slipping to the floor and thinking if the Germans counterattack it's all over. At that point, I couldn't care less.

Of course, when the Quartermaster supply does get water to us in Jerry cans we all pass out again *on water*.

I'm sent back to the hospital, thank goodness.

Someone figures out how dumb this is, having a guy with a sling, drunk and with a bandaged hand and hernia operation walking around. So they put me in a truck, drive me to the river and put me on a boat to cross it. They're ferrying equipment and stuff back and forth, now. They ship me back like a sack of beans, put me on another truck, still no ambulance, and drive me to a hospital.

5. MEN AT WAR

RUSSIAN ROULETTE

The hospital is in Metz. It's a long ride and I'm really feeling rotten, upset stomach and in shock, probably also still drunk from all the champagne. I stay in the field hospital there for two weeks, during which time I read in *Stars and Stripes* that the Soviets are advancing on Berlin. I'm thinking this is the way to run a war, as a spectator, in a bed.

I come back to my outfit on the line just in time, by two days, to meet the Russians. This is the great thing everybody's been preparing for and afraid of. Any German prisoners we have who speak English try to convince us that the Russians won't stop, they'll go right through us.

These Soviets we meet are from Mongolia. They wear fur hats with flaps, not helmets. The only things I can compare them to are teddy bears, or a freshman football team on the way to a game. At the same time they're deadly dangerous.

We share guard posts. The first time I'm on post with one we only smile a lot. There's no way we can communicate. At the end of two hours, one of their trucks comes by to pick up this guy and leave off his replacement.

I'll never forget it; they're picking up these Russian soldiers at different posts. They only slow down, not stop, and these guys try to jump over the tailgate into the back of the truck. But the Russians on the flat bed of the truck push them off. Then the soldiers laugh, pick themselves up out of the dust, run after the truck with ear flaps flapping and are pushed to the ground again. They keep running after the truck until they catch up. Everybody in the truck is laughing and drinking. This happens two or three times while I'm watching and no one seems to get mad, they're all still laughing.

I think they're so glad to have beaten the Germans after the incredible five years of horror they've gone through, they feel nothing can hurt them. Or maybe this is the way they are naturally. I hope I never need to know.

These wild men are issued about a litre of vodka

a day, a canteen full, and they drink it in great gulps and insist we drink it, too. Well, I'd never seen or tasted vodka in my life. Champagne and applejack are like water compared to this stuff. Every day, we're all half looped, and they're *completely* looped, looped and laughing.

In the US Army we have very strict rules about when you can and when you can't fire your rifle. You just can't shoot when you feel like it. These Russians are shooting anything that moves. Also, they're deep into loot and rape.

I don't know why the German women don't hide more than they do. These guys run them down the way you would a deer or a rabbit, shouting and hollering the whole way. Seduction you can't call it. It's rape. Most times, they pull them into a doorway rather than do it out on the street, but not always. The women are begging us to protect them from these beasts. We try, but the Russians point their rifles at us. There's no question that they'll shoot. We're just other targets of opportunity. I begin to think those German prisoners were right.

Also, of course, the same women are taking cigarettes and chocolate from the GIs who are doing their own somewhat more subtle seduction scene, as close to rape as you can get, but not too much rampant violence.

I'm nineteen and I'm really losing confidence in human beings. My morale was pretty low before, but here I am watching all kinds of mayhem going on, things I never even heard of, dreamed of, had nightmares about. With these guys, both Russians and Americans, it isn't just fornication. They're degrading these women, passing them on to each other. I won't go into the details, but it's worse than anyone can imagine.

And no one is controlling this. There are no MPs up with us, the officers, by this time, are as afraid of the non-coms and enlisted men as they are of the enemy. The war is almost over. Some of the officers have been okay, only doing their duty, but others have been mean or tough for no reason, just power mad. These hard-nose guys are mostly in hiding now, hiding from their own troops.

It's terrible. One time, an old German man comes up to me on guard, absolutely trembling and he has a camera. The rule is, all Germans are to turn in their cameras. I don't know why, and I didn't even know about this rule.

He's trying to push off the camera on me and makes me take it. I think he's trying to sell it to me. I don't want a camera, I don't have any use for a camera. I can hardly carry what I have.

Besides, I have no film. But he keeps begging me to take his camera. I offer him some cigarettes, some candy, but he won't take anything. He's practically crying. I take the camera just to shut him up and get him away from the other guys. I sit down on a piece of rubble to have a look. He runs away. It's a beautiful, old, folding bellows camera. It's one of the few things I manage to get home. Until my house burned down, I kept it on my desk to remind me of how brutal and cruel this war is, how helpless the non-combatants are.

RAPE RAP

Finally, the Russians are pulled out. Some kind of settlement is made between the Soviets and the Americans, where they occupy certain areas and we occupy others. Our outfit winds up in a town called Plauen in what used to be East Germany. There aren't many buildings standing, I don't think there's a pane of glass in the whole town. It's a shambles, absolute rubble.

But this looting and raping starts again. I'm Sergeant of the Guard for about ten men in my squad. These are guys I know. They're in my squad. We eat together, laugh together, are scared together. The Russians are gone, but something appears to have broken down when the Russians were here. The guys start thinking 'If they can do it, so can we.' It seems the way many people are, they tend to follow whatever's going on, no matter how bad it might be. Look at boxing, or spectators at football games today, or even basketball, a supposed non-contact sport. It's vicious, violent and everyone is cheering them on.

I can see how what we call the Holocaust happened. It's a weakness in human beings, all human beings, that we must guard against. The herd instinct is strong in most people and they will follow a leader, in almost any insane programme, no matter how inhuman, just because he's the leader and other people are doing it. People who would never think of doing things like burning, gassing people, on their own, find themselves doing what they are told, no matter how cruel, vicious, murderous it might be. And, it's just because *the rest of the people* are doing it.

Look at the French in their revolution, at the Inquisition in Spain, at the pogroms against Jews in Russia, the campaign against the Kulaks, the murders by Mao in China, the white men in America against the Afro-Americans or the indigenous Amerindians. History is filled with these horrible lapses from acceptable human behaviour. Our natural survival systems collapse in our fears. Civilization as we know it fails, the barriers fall, and the worst aspects in human nature are revealed. The façade of civilization is eliminated.

These are the thoughts that run through my mind. I'm finding it hard to hang on.

We're guarding the weirdest things. For example, someone has come down in a parachute and the parachute is hooked up in a tree. We're guarding the parachute, I guess because the silk is valuable and they don't want it stolen, or maybe it's just to give us something to do, hopefully, hopelessly, to keep us out of trouble.

In the cellars of destroyed buildings are stored all kinds of valuable merchandise. It's supposed to be protected from looting by our own soldiers and the German civilians who are still there. There are no German soldiers. They've been pressed back, are still involved in fighting the Russians and being gathered in by the thousands, as prisoners.

We're guarding a lumber yard. A bunch of valuable seeming stuff in a cellar under rubble is to be guarded by us. But we're spread out pretty thin from post to post. I'm supposed to go around on my tour of guard duty and see that everybody is at their post, not asleep or anything. It's late afternoon, we're doing four on and two off.

I'm out on my rounds. I come to the ones who are guarding a cellar with fancy clothes in it. They have beautiful silk scarves, I don't think they were made in Germany, I don't know where they were made, and there are no tags on them. But they're paisley type silk scarves so I dump the water out of a 'liberated' German canteen and just start stuffing those scarves in, tying them one onto the other, like elephants on parade at a circus. I keep stuffing them in. I manage to stuff about seventy scarves into a single canteen, then screw the top on. I have my own canteen for water. This canteen, with the scarves, I put in my duffel bag. I actually get these home to my mother, sister and girlfriend. For years thereafter they have absolutely gorgeous silk scarves. My excuse is, it's German loot. We're allowed to take things like canteens and such stuff as souvenirs of war and ship them home. But, I also ship home a German camouflage jacket and a dress sword I'd taken from a German officer, and the scarves.

It's easy to lose respect for yourself but that's what war does, maybe that's what it's supposed to do. I'm following the herd, 'If they can do it, so can I.'

I go over to these two GIs who are supposedly on guard. They have a couple of women down in the cellar under all the rubble and are doing the obvious with great glee. I'm pissed.

'Get these women out of there, you two. I'm going to tour the rounds one more time and when I come back they'd better be gone.'

I'm really playing Sergeant, somebody has to. I go back to where the GIs who are not on guard are hanging out under the parachute. It's the most comfortable of the guard posts. There's a little overhang left on one building, so we can duck under it if it rains.

'Pete, I'm going out to check if those guys really did get rid of those women.'

After a while I walk back over and the guys are carrying out my orders, but slowly, very slowly. The women have gotten dressed and are just coming out. They need to come up out of a slanted cellar door type thing. It's heavy, it isn't just made of wood, it's steel. The whole cellar might have been some kind of bomb shelter.

So the women go through the gate out onto the street, afraid of me. They start running.

And who should come rolling down the street? Who would believe it? It's the General of our whole division, a man named General Collier. With him is his son who is a Major, also his adjutant, a classic case of nepotism. It means he gets to stay with Daddy all the time. There's a lot of resentment within the officers of our division about this particular arrangement. General Collier is quite an old man – maybe he wasn't – but he seemed old to me then. Even for a division commander, he's old.

They stop the jeep and the General sends his son over to find out what's going on and why these two women are running away from the post.

Just then, the GIs, who *should* be on the post, come tearing out. They're dressed, but they don't have their helmets on, and they don't have their rifles. In other words, by military standards, they're semi-dressed.

Wow, what a set-up for a court martial! Here we go again. It happens to be a time when everyone is getting all upset with ideas of 'fraternisation'. By this, they generally mean getting close to the German women. In England, they showed us movies about German Frauleins who are shown dancing to accordion music, dressed in long skirts and skimpy blouses pushing their boobs up. Later, these same German women are shown stabbing GIs in the back or passing on information, or poisoning GIs in their coffee or beer. The movies were almost as bad as the VD films they showed us in boot camp. We all had a big laugh and the officer in charge kept stopping the film and hollering at us.

Fraternising must have been happening every-where. The trouble is, right now they're looking for a good case of fraternisation to build up a court martial and scare everybody. We look like just the kind of example they're searching for, but, at first, they seem to let it go by.

When I get those two jerks back to the home guard post I *really* play Sergeant and give them hell. I tell them they're getting as bad as the Russians. I mean it and I believe it.

But, we are *actually* all reamed out, notes are taken. There is going to be a court martial about this after all. The Sergeant of the Guard, that's me, and these two guys are hauled in and put under guard. We can't go anywhere. We're confined to quarters. The quarters are not very impressive; we're in a mouldy cellar.

A summary court martial is set up and we hang around. They send us a lawyer who's supposed to defend us. He's a Lieutenant and is scared to death of Collier. Major Collier, the son, is going to be a witness and sort of prosecutor. I'm too young and ignorant of the dangers to be concerned enough about a really serious military court martial. I don't know what's really going on, but we decide we don't want this Lieutenant defending us, he's going to do more harm than good, so we don't tell him anything. But we work out a plan.

They decide not to court martial me. I was Sergeant of the Guard, I saw it all and so I'm to be a witness. The guys in trouble work out a scenario with me. We say I'd just been there less than an hour before and there were no women on this post. It's very hot down there in the cellar and that's why they didn't have their helmets and field jackets on. I'm there because I'm manning the cellar door while they're down doing an inspection of the post. It's a very flimsy kind of excuse but we work out a couple of tricks. We know the Major's not very smart.

For the court martial, there's to be a bird colonel on the court. They're all big brass. They've taken a building that isn't in too bad shape, cleaned it out, and are using it as a sort of courtroom. They have a long table with chairs for all the officers. The deposition is made by Major Collier as to what he has seen and he is straight, trying to say exactly what happened. The officer in charge, the Colonel, calls our assigned Lieutenant to have him speak and he does just what we expected he would do. He repeats almost exactly what Major Collier says, agreeing with him, even though he saw nothing. At the same time, he's making excuses for us, in terms of 'what these men have been through' and so on.

I'm called to testify. It isn't a regular civil trial. There are only two witnesses; me and Major Collier. I ask if I can question Major Collier. The Colonel nods his head.

'Major Collier, were the gates open, closed, or partially open when you arrived?'

He says, 'They were completely open.'

I say, 'There were no gates.' And there weren't.

I get him to admit he's hardly seen the women. I tell how they were a mother and her little girl looking for fire wood and the men on guard had just chased them off when the General arrived.

Now, the court martial board is against Major Collier because of his relationship to his father. After we'd gone through several of these little scenarios, where it becomes obvious Collier hadn't really seen anything, he's well befuddled. The Colonel in charge of the court martial stands up, scraping his chair against the wooden floor as he does so.

'It seems to me, Gentlemen of the court, the evidence for this court martial is not sufficient and has not been properly gathered.'

He looks around at everyone at the table, they all nod their heads. Then, just like that, we're dismissed. Well, the poor Major who was hoping to get his oak leaf, doesn't, and our guys are exonerated. We go out and have a really big K ration celebration afterwards.

ROLIN CLAIRMONT

When I first came back to K Company, I'd been assigned as a scout to the second platoon, I guess because I'd been in I&R. I'm assigned along with a new replacement, named Rolin Clairmont. Since we're the two new arrivals, we're tent mates, as if we ever got to sleep in tents instead of wet holes.

We get to know each other reasonably well. He's tall, at least six three and comes from Bordertown, New York. Before the army, he worked with his father taking hunters into upper New York State and even up into Maine to hunt. Most times they'd fly in. Rolin and his father live on a lake in New York State and they have a plane with pontoons. Rolin has been flying planes illegally since he was thirteen or fourteen years old and knows a lot about them. He also knows a lot about shooting and hunting.

He makes a good tent/hole mate. Most of the people in K Company are from the South, but he turns out to be better than the southerners at being southern. He's had much experience with rifles, hunting of all kinds, from deer and bear, to small game hunting; squirrels, rabbits. He also knows how to build a still, and he can speak French. He tells me he speaks Canadian French. We're not that far into Germany and most of the civilians speak French or German, or both. It's an intermediate, no-man's kind of land.

There's an interesting thing about border zones, in Europe, anyway. They always seem to be much more sleazy, run down, compared to the rest. It's almost as if everything stops moving and working right around the border. This is the kind of area we're in, and putting the war on top of that, it's quite shabby.

When Rolin comes up to K Company, we're in battalion reserve. But two days later we're moved on to Neuendorf, replacing L Company. It's been medium hard according to them, they're going back, and of course they exaggerate, telling us how awful it is and trying to scare us. They say things like, 'You'll be sorry', or 'Take a last look at the world' – all those kinds of usual things.

It's after midnight when we move into the line, so we're slipping and stumbling around, going into holes that are already dug and mucked up. We're two hours on and four off, but when you're off four, you're not really in comfort; you're in another hole, which is dug up against a wall. However, that hole feels like practically going home compared to the outpost hole Rolin and I are sharing guard on. Our hole is the farthest forward, closest to the Germans. It's maybe forty to a hundred yards out from the hole against the wall.

We're out there and we rotate with each other three or four times. Nothing's really happening. I'll never know how the army decides when to move and when not to move. Luckily, in the part of the world we're in, we are neither in attack nor in retreat. I imagine it's a question of getting supplies up or somebody making up his mind.

Then when we charge out and do an attack, we'll settle down to wait again, right after. It's a strange kind of business. It changes later but this is the way it is then. We're taking a bit of territory, then consolidating, taking a bit more, consolidating again.

Rolin and I are out in our hole. It's a pretty good spot right at the edge of the forest looking down a long hill with a stream at the bottom, and then the hill goes up the other side and there's another forest edge over there. That's about four or five hundred yards away. We know the Germans are in the forest. We don't know exactly where, we try to keep an eye out for them but they aren't about to reveal their positions and we aren't going to reveal ours either. We just assume they know where we are but aren't doing anything any more than we are.

We're always careful, we don't stick our heads up and we don't rustle around and make noise. It's a good position to change guard because we have cover almost all the way to the hole and then there's a slight drop going toward the forest. I imagine that's why they dug it here.

Anyway, when we change guard, we come in and the other guys go out, hardly exchanging a word unless something important has happened, and hardly anything has, generally. After that, we'll sit a while to see if any Germans have seen us make the change. Again, it's sort of like 'hide and seek'. Rolin and I are out there a little over an hour into a four hour guard. Night guards are two. Suddenly two German soldiers come out of nowhere, walking right across in front of us. We figure they must be lost or crazy. They come out of the forest on the other side, walking down the hill. They're strolling along the stream with their guns on their shoulders as if there's no war going on at all. We both immediately lift our rifles and release the safeties.

I'm waiting to see Rolin's hunting skills when it comes to real combat. It's a terrible thing to say, but you don't want to take any unnecessary chances. The proper, warlike, military thing to do is to shoot these two guys and duck down, hoping nobody saw you shoot.

It's as bad as that, but that's the way it is. You're not going to shout and stand up yelling, 'Give up. We've got you covered.' You're not about to go down that hill and chase them either. You're just going to shoot them and duck down as fast as possible. Also, you're not going to let them just go by, this is the enemy after all. The sad thing is, we have an obligation to do our part. They're just making the kind of mistake I could easily make myself. I have a rotten sense of direction.

After a minute, it looks to me as if they're sort of coming toward us at a diagonal. They come down to the stream, a small stream, find some rocks and cross it. They must be really lost. They're going at a slow pace with their rifles still slung on their shoulders but they're getting closer and closer.

I'm thinking, 'Boy this guy Clairmont really is a hunter, he never fires until he's ready.' He keeps looking over at me and I keep looking at him. I can see he's getting more and more nervous. I am too. I swear they aren't more than fifty yards away and we can hear them talking.

He turns to me and whispers, 'Would you give a fire order, please?'

I realise he's thinking he's on a rifle range. You aren't allowed to fire on a rifle range unless you have a firing order.

'For Christ's sake Rolin, open up, Fire!' I yell.

Clairmont takes the front one, and I take the back one. They go down twisting and squirming, then are still. We duck down and wait to see what's going to happen. Maybe there are other Germans and they'll start shooting, but all is quiet

Well, I'll never know to this day why those two Germans were strolling around as if there was no war going on. The thing I remember most is the control Clairmont had standing there, waiting for a firing order. It was a premonition of things to come.

A FLIGHT OF FANCY

Rolin and I get to be good buddies. He's a chess nut and has a small portable chess set we play on. We share easily and, except for Rolin's stinky feet and his size, he's a perfect tent mate. Within a few weeks, while we're in company reserve, I manage to pick up another small shrapnel wound in my shoulder. Flying shrapnel in those days is almost as common as wasps. I'm sent back to the field hospital and they take it out and put in a few stitches.

Once again, I milk this little wound as long as I can to stay off the line. And I get my second purple heart. We're beginning to hear rumblings of a point system for discharging when the war is over. This purple heart is worth five points to me toward discharge.

When I finally come back to the outfit the guys have had some pretty rough stuff again. In particular, they've had a bad time in a place they call 'the crossroads'. It's like people talking all the time about a movie you haven't seen. It's common with soldiers to name battles as a place personal to themselves. These battles I'm sure have different names and numbers in the military records where such things are kept, but to us, they are private property. When someone is hit or killed we refer to the situation as 'he got hit at the crossroads', or whichever private landmark is nominated for that bad time.

By being in the hospital, I've missed the 'battle of the crossroads'. Because there are so many casualties, and because Rolin is such a natural soldier, he's been made a squad leader and a staff sergeant while I've been gone. He wants me for his assistant squad leader. Normally the squad leader and the assistant don't share the same tent or hole, but we pull it off.

For Rolin, the war is like some kind of game, a combination of chess and Russian roulette. He likes it! Of course, I'm still scared out of my mind by the whole thing. So we have a sort of symbiotic relationship in which he plays war hero and I'm his audience. We begin taking patrols together, just the two of us. This is also not the way it should be done. But Rolin always volunteers us for some of the most treacherous patrols and I go along because he's so persuasive. That's how I get into my second most ridiculous event of the war, after that D-3 day. And it involves a small airplane again, my little personal history repeating itself.

We're roaming around on a vague patrol, looking for an L4 airplane that's been shot down, not too different from the one I was dumped out of at the start of my personal war.

Rolin is acting as combination scout and squad leader. We're in an area where there's been tons of artillery thrown against the enemy, directed by little Piper cubs called L4 artillery observers. The Germans keep trying to shoot them down, but it must be harder than one would think because it's rare they get one. But this time they do, and Rolin swears he saw where it went down.

We, as ground troops, are not too happy having these planes fly over top of us because they give the Germans an idea as to where we are on the ground. Also, there's some shrapnel fallout from the ack-ack of anti-aircraft guns.

Our patrol, as designed by Rolin, is to see if we can locate this L4. He's convinced it's been shot down in something of a no-man's land between the two meandering front lines. Everything is fairly fluid right now.

It's coming on to early spring and Rolin is all hopped up. We're just wandering and, as usual, I'm scared half to death. I'm trying to keep track with my compass so we can get back, shooting azimuths about every ten minutes.

'You don't need to do that, Will,' Rolin tells me. 'I know my way back. Remember, I used to take these Wild Bill hunters into the deep woods of New York and Maine. I know just where we are.'

'Yeah, but do you know where we're going?' I ask. 'Remember those two Krauts we shot, just wandering around? Something like that could happen to us, too.'

About five minutes later we look out from the edge of a wood, and sure enough, see that L4 we're looking for. We sit for about half an hour trying to see if anybody's around, either the guys who were flying it, or some Kraut keeping watch on it. We don't see a thing.

'Hell, I'm getting tired of just sitting around, Will. You cover me.'

With that, he's off with his rifle unslung, moving toward the airplane. I have an M1, I lost my carbine with the filed off sear somewhere in the trip back to the hospital. I keep the rifle lined up on him, scanning as he goes.

He walks right up to the plane, turns back, and waves for me to come on down. I move toward him cautiously, expecting someone to pick me off. God, how do I get in situations like this?

Rolin's all excited. He's sitting in the cockpit by the time I get there. He wants me to give the prop a twist to start the engine. I've never done anything like that, so he jumps out and demonstrates a few times how to do it, with both hands, pull hard clockwise, then jump out of the way. I do that and he's inside trying to get the motor started but nothing happens. He smiles and jumps out.

'No gas. Could those idiots have just let this thing go down because they didn't fill it with gas?'

He looks in back of the plane and finds two Jerry cans full of high octane gas. He passes them out to me.

'I'll bet some lucky Kraut bastard managed to put a bullet hole into the gas tank, or maybe one of those puffs of anti-aircraft smoke we see actually had some shrapnel in it. So there's most likely a hole and the gas drained right on out. Boy, those guys in this bird must have been scared shitless. I don't see any blood in the cockpit so either they got back somehow, or the Krauts took them prisoner.'

While he's saying this, he's looking around under the airplane. He pushes his finger into a hole.

'Here it is. Those guys were lucky this thing didn't just blow up on them or burst into flames.'

'Let's get out of here, Rolin. Those Germans could have a guard on this plane. They must have seen it come down, too.'

'What, leave a perfectly good plane out here in this field because of an iddy biddy hole? Let's see if we can get this baby off the ground again.'

He's already crawled back into the fuselage and is pounding with a wrench against the inside of the gas tank. He tells me to put the butt of my rifle against the hole on the outside. In five minutes he has that hole pounded out just about smooth.

'We're lucky,' he says. 'The gas stopped the bullet or piece of shrapnel, or whatever it was, so there's only one hole. Wait a minute.'

He's searching through his field jacket pockets. He pulls out two sticks of gum and starts chewing one. He gives me the other.

'My ten year old brother sent these. He knows how much I like to chew bubble gum. Boy, he'll appreciate the way we're going to use it.'

When we have the gum chewed up, he starts sticking it down on the remains of the hole. He smears it tight into the cracks of the hole pressing it inside and out.

'Man, I hope gum isn't soluble in gasoline, but it doesn't really matter. We probably won't be going that far.'

So we fill the tank with the two Jerry cans and Rolin gets into the cockpit again. After five or six tries, I spin the propeller right and the motor turns over. Rolin motions me into the plane.

'Come on, Will, we're going to have some fun.'

I've never been in an airplane before except for those parachute jumps at Benning, that channel-hopping ride where I was pushed out, and the short ride with my Dad. But I climb in. In some strange way, I'm mesmerised.

Rolin taxies the plane uphill to the edge of the forest. He turns it around, guns the motor and starts going downhill at full speed. I duck down expecting we're going to crash at any minute. Imagine an infantryman being killed in a little airplane like this in the middle of a field. I can hardly think. Rolin is laughing.

He clears the trees on the other side of the field by about two feet and we're in the air. He waggles the wings for fun.

'Stop it, Rolin. I can't take it. You'll have me upchucking all over this thing.'

We're heading out over the German lines because that's the direction the hill went down.

'Rolin, you're going the wrong way. Turn around.'

'Can't, not yet. The wind's all wrong.'

Just then we start getting bursts of anti-aircraft guns, 88s as far as I can tell, bursting all around us. I'm ducking down in the cockpit and Rolin's grinning and pulling that plane higher, then he practically tips it over in a tight turn which almost throws me against the door and we're heading back to where we've come from. The ack-ack lets up a bit. I climb up from where I was, practically on the floor.

'I don't think we're finished, Will, unless you can figure how to use the radio in this baby. Our own guys will be taking pot shots at us soon.'

I reach for the radio dials and start spinning them but I'm getting nothing. This is like a bad dream repeating itself. I shout into it, hoping there's somebody out there somewhere listening. At least the light on the dial is lit. But then it comes, more puffs all around us and the ping of shrapnel on the plane.

'Higher Rolin, can't you get this thing any higher?'

We're just skimming over the trees.

'Sure, but if I get any higher those fools with the seventy five mm guns will have a better shot at us. If I keep low, they don't have enough time to get a bead on us.'

So we skim along, just missing tops of trees or hills and in about five minutes it stops. Rolin still keeps flying just about the height of telephone poles. He's concentrating.

'Keep on trying the radio, Will. We've got to let them know we're friendly aircraft, not some Kraut in an L4. Look at the gas gauge too, will you? I can't take my eyes away from what's in front of me.'

I look and it's about half full. So we skip along over ridge and forest, watching lines of troops moving forward or camped or scattering in fear as we swoop low over them. Rolin can't help waving his wings at some of them in a line along a road, especially the tanks. I think it's his way of thumbing his nose. I keep my eye on the gas gauge and watch it slowly swing to the left, wondering what Rolin has in mind.

'Will, I think we can get this old crate so far behind the lines it won't be worth their while to ship us all the way back to our outfits. It'll be fun, anyway.'

It isn't half an hour after this statement that the

motor starts to cough and we begin losing altitude.

'Keep an eye out for another open field, Will, or at least some kind of ploughed field where we can set this thing down. I saw two small airfields a ways back, but I don't think we can make it to them.'

We keep chugging, missing, coughing and losing altitude. At the last moment, we do come in on a field of what looks like wheat. It's flat and almost long enough. Rol bears down and takes good aim. I brace my hands against the airplane's equivalent to a dashboard and jam my feet against the floor.

Just as we're about to touch the ground, Rol pulls the nose up so we settle back slightly and hit with hardly a serious bump. I'm so excited I applaud.

'You should see me land our seaplane on lakes not much bigger than puddles. Taking off again is the hard part.'

We're climbing out of the plane when about twenty men in foreign uniforms come running out at us with rifles. I begin to think we might have gone the wrong way, after all.

We lean our rifles against the plane and put our hands up. I can't understand a word of what this mob is shouting at us. But Rolin starts shouting back. They surround us and stop. They jabber away with Rolin. Rolin is smiling. It seems we've landed in the middle of a supply dump for a French Canadian outfit.

Rolin apparently explains everything and they start speaking to me in English. French-English, but I can understand enough.

They take us back to the command tent. I can't figure out the rank from the insignia, but this is medium high brass. They talk to Rolin, then the top guy turns to me.

'Is this true you found this craft in an open field, repaired it and flew it here?'

'That's right, Sir.'

'And where is your regular outfit right now?'

I point over my shoulder.

'Up there, Sir. We're infantry. We flew until we were sure we were in friendly territory.'

He laughs and the others are laughing with him.

'You practically flew back to England. Where'd you learn to fly like that, buddy? What do you think we can do with you now, anyway?'

I speak up before Rolin gets a chance.

'We could help with your work. Just notify our outfits by radio that we're here so they won't think we've deserted or something or that we're missing in action. I'm tired of being in the infantry anyway.'

I can feel this isn't going over very well. The men mutter to themselves in French. There are crowds of soldiers at the open flap of the tent. The officer speaks up again.

'Sergeant Clairmont is asking to be transported back to your regiment as soon as possible. I'm afraid we must do that. You cannot stay here.'

So, thanks to Rolin and his gung ho war attitude that's just what happens. It's astounding how far we've flown. We're almost a week moving in truck convoys over crowded roads. I remember with sentimental memory how easily we'd flown over this same route going the *right* way. Now we start hearing the crumping sound of big artillery, then the smaller sound of anti-tank guns and anti-craft, then the thump of mortars, finally, the crack and whistling of small arms. We're home! We're back in K Company. All that for nothing.

We're surrounded when we get back. It seems they did send out missing in action telegrams to our families. They countermand those as fast as possible, but I'm sure not fast enough to stop a lot of worrying. I find out later that they came one day after the other, the countermand first. This was obviously confusing and not very convincing to our parents.

Rolin's using his hands, acting out our flight for

everybody. He makes it sound even more exciting than it was, if that's possible. I only listen. The amazing part is that Rolin is sent back to Division Headquarters where they give him a silver star for saving the plane.

DOWNHILL SLIDE

Too soon, I'm squad leader again. Then I get just another little wound below my knee, enough to go back to the field hospital again. There's a small piece of shrapnel embedded in there so they take it out, sew it up and put another little bandage on it. That's my third purple heart. I feel like a kid at school who keeps falling down on the playground, gets sent to the nurse who puts some mercurochrome on the cut, and is sent back out to play. The people at the hospital are getting to know me. After the airplane thing, I'm something of a celebrity.

When we were together before I got wounded, before the airplane folly, Rolin was always reading his Bible. He was a great Bible reader. He doesn't talk about it, but when he has a little free time he reads the Bible. He makes no big thing about it and I don't say anything because it's his business.

But, when I come back from the hospital again, Rolin's Bible is nowhere in sight, and he's a different guy. That little bit of war hero celebrity has somehow released something inside him. He's taken to drinking, gambling – the whole thing. He's on his way to being a classic, true blue, non-com.

Since I've gotten back, our situation is even scarier. We are now attacking the Siegfried Line. The German bunkers are in that very complicated zigzag pattern. They're around a town called Reuth, which is the control centre for that portion of the Siegfried Line. It's why we're held up.

I don't know what we're waiting for, but the Germans are hardening their positions. They even have Mark 2 Tiger tanks come up and are preparing for a big assault. Our S2, Regimental Intelligence, wants to know as much as possible about what the Germans are doing, so we're pushing our forward posts further and further forward. We'll dig a hole and be there for a day, half a day, then wait for nightfall to move forward and dig in again. After the war we could get jobs as grave diggers.

To go out and take the forward post is quite a trip. It's far and we're all dragging, deeply fatigued. Also, we're short of men again because of some action I'd happily missed. We're on four and off four, which means we don't get much sleep. Normally the Sergeant of the Guard, Rolin, and the Corporal of the Guard, me (even though I'm now a Sergeant), don't stay on guard duty together, but the platoon is about half its normal strength and from long guards, day and night, just about totally wiped out. So, Rolin in his usual impossible way, suggests the two of us take the king four hour guard at the forward post from midnight to four in the morning – the worst one – to give everybody else a break.

I'm not happy with this idea. It's a hard guard to stand. He's afraid someone out there on post will fall asleep and we could be overrun. There's a lot of patrolling by the Germans these nights. It's the type of situation which is very uncomfortable, very spooky. Everybody's nervous and jumpy, especially me.

So we go out and work our way through the series of holes leading out there. The two guys we relieve are nervous wrecks. They swear there are Germans all around them, but they can't see any because it's so dark.

The moon is mostly overcast. Once we're out there we're able to see a bit, but not enough. It's farm country – open, with bits of woods. There's probably a mile separating the two towns, Reuth, where the Germans are, and our town, Neuendorf. Both towns are thoroughly turned into rubble. Our platoon is staying in a cellar in the centre of it all, a smoke filled, smelly cellar.

We make it out to the point post and we're taking turns, one kind of keeping his eye open and watching for movement, while the other sits down in the hole and meditates on life and death. I sit there hunched up, there isn't all that much room in a foxhole and we don't have much to talk about.

In this foxhole, we have a fire step. Whoever dug this hole has done a good job. When you're standing on the fire step your head is up above the dirt piled around the hole and if you're the reckless type, you can rest your arms on the parapet of the foxhole. If the dirt's piled right you have a fair view for a line of fire and a reasonable amount of protection.

This night, even though I'm now a Sergeant again, for this patrol, I'm toting a BAR (a Browning Automatic Rifle). I want us to have some fire power if things go as wrong as I think they're going to go. We don't have a BAR Assistant so I'm not only toting the BAR, which is a heavy weapon, but I'm carrying the reserve ammunition for it in a thick webbing belt around my waist. I also have a bandoleer of 30 calibre clips around my neck. This is usually the job of the BAR Assistant who would normally be carrying an M1.

I have the BAR set up on the parapet with a little tripod. This isn't always the case, but a BAR tends to rise as one shoots because it's a rifle firing fifteen consecutive shots automatically. One just needs to hold the trigger tight and the weapon down.

It's my turn on guard, when I see a German patrol going across our field of view. I see them moving, covering each other. They apparently don't know we're there. This is a Tiger type patrol, out looking for trouble or a prisoner. This, if it weren't for Rolin, is just fine with me. Let them look. I'll help them find me. I won't mind being a prisoner. I'm tired of this war, feeling I'm running out of luck, but the trouble is, giving up is hard to do. You can't be sure they won't just shoot you, kill you, without asking too many questions.

So I nudge Rolin and he stands up, he's been asleep. Some people can sleep anywhere – Rolin is one – I'm not. He sees the patrol and tenses up. This is not the tension of fear, this is the tension of the hunter, the cat on the prowl. Before I know it, Rolin is giving me instructions.

'We're going to get these guys. There are eight of them and we can get them all.'

He points out to me, quietly, where each one of them is. His idea is we pick off the ones at the back first. He's really hunting. That means they'll have farther to run when they realise we're up here and have automatic fire.

He says, 'Squeeze off shots, Will, try not to shoot more than one at a time. We'll pick them off from the back, or if you need to, you can keep sweeping automatic, you have plenty of ammunition, it's up to you. I'll knock off anybody who gets out of your range before they have a chance.'

So, this is our basic plan; he has organised a hunt. I slump up there on the parapet and he gives me the signal to fire, my knees are shaking. I'm shooting at the most two hundred yards, which is a good distance for a BAR to be accurate. I fire off one shot, and the man goes down. Then I swing to get the next one and the BAR jams! BARs are known for this.

I start emergency procedures knowing there are

seven guys out there who know where we are. They're either charging toward us or running away; I can't even look I'm so busy. I'm pushing in the clip and jamming it tight, pulling back the bolt and doing all the emergency procedures you do when your BAR jams. I keep trying to pull the trigger and nothing's happening, I reach in my belt for a new clip.

In the meantime Rolin is standing up, he's tall, he's standing right down in the hole with his feet against the back wall and is firing the way I should be firing. Boom, pah, boom, boom. He has a full seven shots plus one in the chamber. He fires one after the other, well spaced, while I'm sweating like crazy over the damned BAR. Then I think he's run out of ammunition. He pulls out a new clip; but he does it real slow and easy.

'Hurry up Rolin, they're going to get away or they're going to get us! Are they coming toward us or are they running away?'

He smiles in the dark. 'Well they started running away and I began picking off the ones in front as they ran; then they turned back toward us so I concentrated on the ones who were in the front as they came toward us. I think I got them all.'

I look out. Without missing one shot he's

downed every one of them! A chill runs through me.

There are foxholes to either side of us, but much farther back. We have a telephone out there with us in our hole going directly to the CP, but it doesn't go to either side. Those guys aren't yelling or anything, they don't want to give away their positions. At Rolin's instructions I crank up our phone.

They switch me to Captain Wall and I tell him what's happened.

'How many in the patrol?'

'About eight. Clairmont shot them all except one I got before the BAR jammed.'

'Hell's bells. Go out and check to see if they're all dead, take a prisoner if any are alive. Regiment is interested in who and what's in front of us. Find out who it is if you can. If they're all dead, cut off the insignias so we can verify what outfit we're facing.'

In the meantime, Rolin has already gone out there on his own, no cover! I know by now he's like an old time mercenary soldier.

I hang up the phone and cover him. Nobody moves, he goes to each one, and goes through their pockets, slicing away insignia with his well-sharpened bayonet. I can just about see him because it's dark and after maybe half an hour he comes back. He has a big grin on his face and blood all over his hands. He's like somebody who's just come in from dressing a deer he's shot. For a nice guy he has the most evil grin I've ever seen. Out of one pocket, he takes watches, wallets, rings and so forth. He uses his bayonet to dig a deep hole in the bottom of our foxhole then puts all this loot in it, stomps it down tightly. In his other field jacket pocket, like a saddle bag almost, he has all the insignia and rank that he's ripped off along with two pistols. He left the rifles.

He says, 'I'm going to take all this back, you stay here.'

He leaves his rifle. It's still warm.

I'm figuring there might be a backup patrol and I'm scared to death. He comes out again just about the time our guard duty is supposed to be over. He has the two replacements with him to take our place; they're shaking in their boots. Rolin scoops up the loot he'd stuffed in the hole he dug and sticks it in his pocket, dirt and all. He won't even let these new guys jump in the hole until he's gotten it all out.

When we get back, Captain Wall wants to have my report on what happened, says he wants all the details. I tell him basically how Sergeant

Clairmont stood up and shot down every one of them, while my BAR was jammed.

'Just one rifle load, Sir, seven straight shots. In my opinion he deserves a silver star at least.'

I know that's what he wants me to verify, what had actually happened. He did put in for a silver star but Rolin never got it. He'd had one too recently, I guess. Some Lieutenant probably got it for pissing straight down a hole.

Rolin is the only American I know who's as rough and tough as the Russian-Mongolians, worse than the southerners in a certain way. He's as unafraid and happy-go-lucky as the guys in their floppy hats. He laughs and carries on and drinks anything anybody hands him. The only difference is he never rapes a woman. He doesn't need to. However, he always has a constant supply of candy bars and cigarettes. He has sex appeal or something because German women chase after him. It seemed to me he's indefatigable.

There are some Polish women slave labourers in these German towns and they're hungry for food or anything we can give them – K rations or whatever we have. And they're as hungry for sex as German women. I begin to suspect there might be something wrong with *me*. Sex for the sake of sex has no appeal to me. We can't even talk to these women, they speak some German but no English.

It's like a regular holiday for just about everyone, and it lasts a while because later we're manning road blocks on the autobahn and some of the small roads, as well. Lots of chances to make contacts.

Anybody who passes by, usually on foot, heavily loaded, we demand some identification from, and if they don't have it we send them to the military government guys, and the CIC.

The last I heard of Rolin Clairmont is that when he goes home on furlough, between wars, the German and Japanese, during which they drop the atomic bomb, he goes on a real toot. After having gone through the whole war without a scratch, taking all kinds of risks, he takes his father's airplane, flies it under telephone wires, misses, crashes, and gets twenty-three stitches in his head and a concussion. Well, it should have been enough. I'm sure a psychiatrist could write some kind of paper explaining how Rolin needed to play war to prove something to himself. Maybe they'd say he didn't have enough self-esteem or something, but for Rolin, I think the war was fun. I think he was one of the few people who lived through the damned thing and actually enjoyed it. I also think he was frustrated when we dropped that atom bomb. When we were told at Fort Benning about the beaches we would have charged up just south of Tokyo, it was obvious he was disappointed. What does a civilised society do with a guy like that? I guess sometimes we just put them in jail or an insane asylum.

THE GREAT JEWEL ROBBERY

We finally go through the Siegfried Line and start a great end run across Germany. We're moving so fast they pile us into two ton trucks. We go along faster than tanks. Sometimes, we come to a town and there will be German civilians in them. There's been no chance for the civilian population to evacuate. These towns have never been bombed. Some of them are still there, complete with women and children.

We first do what we call 'clearing' in each town. This means going through each house, cellars and all, seeing that there are no soldiers hiding. As we roll into these towns, armed to the teeth, there are often women at the windows. Some guys just head for the women, some look for booze, wine or schnapps, and some go after silver or gold.

Everybody has his particular loot. We're way ahead of the MPs, so nobody's stopping us.

I get to be real expert at finding where the Germans hide their jewels. Usually they're in dinky safes behind paintings. I blow the locks off with my rifle. My rationale is they've probably stolen all this stuff from the Poles, the French or the Jews from all the countries where they've ravaged, robbed and killed. We think of ourselves as the great liberators, 'liberating' all this loot.

Now I know more about it. I realise I often was taking their personal property and many times this property had sentimental and family value to them. But I was nineteen years old, a scared and unwilling dogface soldier, working myself up to being a mercenary. I didn't want to work the rest of my life if I could avoid it. If I could bring some of this stuff home and sell it, I'd have a real nest egg.

I did learn to pop diamonds and other precious stones from their settings like popcorn. I don't want the settings, just the gems. Diamonds, rubies, emeralds, anything that looks valuable I shove in my field jacket pockets as fast as I can. I abandon the settings, just move right through the houses, one after the other. I don't touch anybody. People are too scared to say much. Sometimes they try to resist, mostly women and old men, but not much. We're worse than the Russians, all right.

Every evening I take these jewels and, using the little cloth patches we use to clean our rifle barrels, sew my day's haul into the inside of my combat field pack.

Finally, after our great wild run, we settle down for a few days. There's one kid in our outfit whose father is a jeweller. He sees what I'm doing and peers over my collection.

'Good God, Wharton, you've got a fortune there! I wish I'd thought of that, it's the smartest thing of all. It's loot you can probably get home.'

He looks carefully through what I have.

'I don't care what fence you go to. That stuff is worth ten thousand dollars or more, easy. And since you don't have the settings, nobody can identify them. Only be careful, wait a while after the war before you try to sell any of it.'

I'm also thinking of putting these gems inside the filter can of a German gas mask. That would be classified as just a souvenir, no trouble. There are quite a few gas masks we've gotten from the Germans. They're a crazy kind of souvenir, almost as crazy as the poor Krauts hauling them all over Europe, but everyone is sending one back, maybe for Halloween they could be used as masks. We'd all ditched the huge packet that was our own gas mask long ago.

I figure I'll take the charcoal out, mix the stones in, then put it back together again. I have my plan all worked out, but I don't get to do it that way.

6. AFTERMATH

CELEBRATION

The war's over on the ninth of May, VE Day they call it. My way of celebrating the war being over is personal and nearly gets me another court martial. Our Captain tells us that at midnight, the war's officially over. We're out in the fields, sleeping in tents, the weather's warm, there isn't much in the way of action. We have our big surprise coming about a week later.

I'm waiting in my tent until the hands of my German officer's watch, with a luminous dial, cross over each other and show midnight. Another piece of war loot. I know some people who have six or seven watches up and down each arm. They have them set for Chicago time, Los Angeles time, New York time, and so forth; spend all their time winding them.

Anyway, just at midnight, I have my M1 standing straight up between my legs, pointing at the V forming the top of our tent. VE day right? Rolin Clairmont's sleeping beside me. I brace the butt tight between my legs and, at the moment of midnight, fire off eight paced shots right through the tent.

I look out our tent flap. The whole camp, *everybody*, comes tearing out; they can't see where the firing's from. People have rifles out and are running around like headless chickens in their skivvies. I come crawling out of our tent and yell, 'Yippee, the war's over. Hooray!'

I think for a minute there someone's going to shoot me, especially Rolin, who's shaking his head as if his ears are falling off.

They jump me, and drag me into the Captain's tent. He's half asleep and half dressed. The platoon explains it to him, all at the same time. In a while he figures it out.

'Wharton, why the hell did you do that? You deserve a section eight!'

'Well, Sir, nobody seemed to be celebrating. Here we are; we're alive. We somehow got through this war. At least we're not going to die in this war, maybe we'll die in another one, somewhere else, who knows. But it's worth celebrating, Sir.'

He stares at me smiling, and gets to laughing. Then the rest of the company starts laughing. Captain Wall doesn't do anything really. I just need to serve an extra guard to make up for the sleep everybody lost. There it is, that's the way I celebrate the end of the war. Little did I know.

FLAME THROWERS

About a week after this it's getting to be summer warm for the first time. It's the kind of weather I thought we'd have when we started this war by landing on those beaches. For months, we've been sleeping in all our clothes, taking our shoes off as usual, tucking them in the bottom of the sack and then being ready to roll at a moment's notice. Now, I'm sleeping in just my shorts and OD undershirt. I don't even have socks on. I'm practically a civilian.

Well, where we are now, it's been quiet for more than a week and we're settled down in a little forest. It's very pleasant, like camping out. The field kitchen's actually caught up with us. I've learned to say '*haben sie eine?*' Fresh eggs we have not had. I'm not really sure where we are, somewhere in what became East Germany.

We're all in our tents, sound asleep. I have my pack at my head, with my loot in it, tucked in at the top of the tent in the little triangular shaped back. I have it tucked up there to be safe. Rolin and I aren't making too big a deal of it. I've made my plan for trying to get these home, I am carrying a Kraut gas mask in my duffel bag, my looting days are over. I feel . . . it's hard to explain, I don't feel guilty about those jewels. I truly feel I'm liberating these stones from the enemy, the Germans. They're the enemy, and we're so conditioned, after all the misery and killing, to think of them that way, not as human beings. What the hell, taking their jewellery is nothing compared to what they've done.

Then, in the middle of the night, there's all kinds of hollering, shooting and shouting. I run out of the tent. At first, I can't figure what it's all about. It looks like German commandos or SS or something, but turns out to be a group of Hitler Youth with their leader wearing a uniform like a boy scout leader and carrying a sword. These are all kids, twelve to fifteen years old at the most, and they have handmade flame throwers, with garden sprays and gasoline. These contraptions are amazingly effective. The little devils are spraying every which way, spraying the tents, spraying the whole camp, hollering and screaming at the same time. They have some small arms, too. I take off like a rabbit, with just my rifle, that's all, and I run barefoot, in my shorts, over the pine needles, doing everything I can to get out of there fast.

We reach another little wood, and they're still running around spraying everything. They also have Jerry cans filled with fuel oil and they spread it around, too, and light that.

When we finally come back after chasing off those kids, most of us naked or only half dressed, we have a hell of a time putting the fires out and saving what equipment we can. Our tent is totally burned and just about everything in it. What I'm interested in is my loot. I go back there and fish around in the charcoal and ashes. There's nothing. I don't know just what happened, but almost everybody's field pack has been taken. I guess wearing them makes the kids feel more like soldiers or something, ready for the next war. Rifles and pistols are left, only the field packs are taken, nothing else, not even the blankets that weren't burned. And with the field packs these kids and their boy scout leader have disappeared into the night. Luckily, I have the canteen with the scarves tied up on the branch of a tree.

Well that was the end of my career as a jewel thief. But some kid must have gotten a nice surprise if he unsewed some of those patches.

MASSACRE

There is a very sad story, and one which I never told my children, for good reason. I still have a hard time facing up to it inside myself. I'm having a hard time trying to get myself to write it. I guess that's why I put it off till last. I want to tell it as honestly as possible.

I'm sent back to the hospital again because I'm still having troubles with dizziness. They do a series of tests but they come back and say there's nothing wrong with me. It takes fifty years for me to find out what's wrong. But the army does an electro-encephalogram, and there is nothing abnormal showing in my brain. They just figure I'm dogging it and send me back to my outfit.

I'm trying to figure when this would have been. It's all so jammed together after all the years. I

246

know it was before the war was over and after the collapse of the German army. It's before the Hitler Youth attack.

I'm put in charge of a company group, a Tiger patrol unit again. This is not I&R, it's an aggressive patrolling group and it's formed more or less independently of the company but is part of it. There are eight of us and we are going out after prisoners. The Germans *want* to surrender, and we give them the chance. It's not much fun, however. If a bunch of them wants to surrender, and there's one hard nose who doesn't want to, he can just open up on us with a burp gun. Too many guys get this far and this is the way the war ends for them.

In general, streams of Germans are dashing as fast as they can toward the West to surrender. They're trying to surrender to Americans by preference, the alternative is the Russians in the East.

So it's a strange time of war, it doesn't last all that long. But we're out on one of these Tiger patrols when a group of Germans, there are ten of them, step out of a wood and want to surrender. They step into a clearing, waving a flag and throw down their rifles. They're a raggedy, loose, sad looking bunch. As soon as the surrender is established, after the rifles are gathered up and they have their hands on their heads, I figure the patrol is over.

I put the fellow who's been in charge of this patrolling group before I came back from the hospital, in control. I want to take a walk by myself to the CP. When I get back there, I sack out in a pup tent without reporting, figuring I can do that later. I'm on the edge of tears. I'm beginning to feel I need to turn myself in to the medics and just say I can't go on, take whatever they do to someone who has combat fatigue.

As I say, things are relatively easy; we've been in the same place for two days and in those times, that's a long time to be in any one place. I don't know why we're here, or what's going on. I'm mentally out of it. The bigger mechanism of the war is beyond me and doesn't really interest me enough. I know it would be easy for me to get killed. I don't care enough any more.

But then, the guys come in and they don't have the prisoners. I'm shocked.

'Where are the prisoners?' I ask the one I put in charge.

'Ah, they tried to escape so we shot the bastards, Sarge,' he answers.

Immediately I don't believe him. I know these guys are really a strange group. But I also know they've been in this anti-tank battalion the whole war, and have never had to fire in anger.

These old time anti-tank guns didn't make any sense any more, so all during the war these guys have just been scared to death, waiting. They've had seventy five mm guns that they've had to haul around behind jeeps and shoot tanks. A seventy-five mm gun has practically no chance of knocking out a German tank. A jeep has no chance of surviving a hit from an eighty eight mm mounted on a tank, either.

With the invention of the bazooka, anti-tank warfare ideas changed completely. The old anti-tank battalions are useless. They'd never really been used and so are finally broken up and distributed. This is how they came to be in this company patrol group. Bad luck for everybody.

I begin to suspect what's happened. I go to Captain Wall, and tell him how I've taken the patrol out and we'd captured ten Germans. I tell him how I came in earlier expecting them to bring the prisoners in. Now, I've found out they didn't bring them in and they say the prisoners tried to escape so I think they shot them. I should have kept my trap shut, not having reported earlier, but I'm scared, angry and not thinking well.

Captain Wall is a decent man. He wants to find

out what really happened out there as much as I do. I'm convinced they've massacred these men. We go out to find out what happened. Several members of the Tiger patrol squad go with us. They are now beginning to intimate what really happened. They start yelling about Malmedy – where Americans who surrendered were shot by Germans – and all the other atrocities of the Germans which are beginning to become known, and so forth.

I realise these are just a bunch of vicious, violent animals and I've done a really wrong thing, leaving them on their own. In court, later on, some turn witness and tell how the squad leader and one of the scouts tortured the Germans, shooting them in the legs, then the arms, before they killed them. One tells how one of the Germans pulled out a wallet with photos of his family and started crying.

Some of them are feeling guilty about it all, but the worst of them are proud of themselves, consider themselves avenging patriots.

We go back to where they've hidden the bodies. They've put them in shallow graves with brush and pine needles raked over so no one would find them until we'd all be off and gone. I vomit when we dig the bodies up. The CO turns white and looks away. He's furious.

He wants to convene a general court martial on this. However, he's told if they do this, the entire massacre will go into the Congressional Record. The officers don't want this in the Congressional Record, a public record that anyone can read. They don't want the American people to know for one thing, and for another they don't want the Germans to know, because it could be used as propaganda to keep soldiers from surrendering.

So instead they make a special court martial out of it. No one really talks too much about what really happened. The guy who's in charge of the patrol, the one I'd replaced, is the one who's really responsible. He instigated and egged on the other members of the patrol into doing it. There are some who really didn't shoot and they give evidence. Everybody is sentenced from two to ten years in Leavenworth, a federal prison, as well as dishonourable discharges, the whole bag.

I'm told by the chief of the court martial that I was responsible, I should have stayed on till the end of the patrol. There was no justification for my having left them. I was in dereliction of duty.

But Captain Wall testifies and protects me pretty well. They break me to private again, take away another six months' salary. No matter what, it doesn't mean anything to me any more. Within a month, Captain Wall has me back as squad leader. We become good friends. What we've shared brings us together.

It's a really bad way to end a war. If there's a good way to end a war I don't know what it is, but this was a bad way to end one.

At the final sentencing, the bastard who got ten years, sees me in the courtyard as they go out. He yells, 'Better watch out Wharton. In ten years you're not safe. I'll have your ass.'

This really upsets the Colonel in charge of the court martial who tells this rotter he's exactly the kind of person the army doesn't want and he's a disgrace to his uniform. They strip him of his stripes in public.

But I'll tell you, when the first two years are over, I'm nervous, then for ten years more I sweat it out. I don't know whether they all served their full terms or not. I want to put that part of my life behind me. The brutality of it all is sickening. How low human beings can come when you take the leash off them. I still have something of this feeling in me. I don't have much confidence in my fellow human beings even sixty years later.

I know how easy it would be to trick the young and everyone else into going off and fighting another stupid, meaningless war. I know how humans will turn on each other, the way cats and dogs will, in the right situation. I know from myself what one can do in the name of greed, in the name of power. These convictions lodge in my soul and have been difficult to shake. They change me.

The main thing I do learn is that I don't ever want vested authority again. For one reason, I feel I'm not the right type of person. I am not responsible enough. For another, I don't really believe in vested authority as such. Any authority I might have, any power *anyone* can have in this life, should be a result of what he or she can do, not power given as the result of a hierarchy. I've lived my life without getting involved in power.

The closest I've come to a power hierarchical structure is when I've been teaching. I did a fairly good job of it. The kids liked me and learned. Then they wanted to move me into school administration. I backed off. That was thirty-five years ago and I quit teaching fairly soon thereafter. Since then, I've only worked for myself, doing the things

I'm good at, not having to tell anyone else what to do.

Of course there are the important people who build the roads, bridges, dams and so forth. In an abstract way they work for us, for all of us. But, in our family, we've never had any servants, I can't take that responsibility. I don't work for anybody myself, and have no one working for me.

At nineteen I made these decisions, and these decisions were from having had this kind of responsibility thrust upon me when I was too young.

7. HOMECOMING

FORT DIX, NEW JERSEY

You now know about my being responsible in a way for the massacre, the shooting and killing of people who had surrendered and the rest of it. Well, after the war I'm sent to Fort Dix. I have enough discharge points to get out, but they have to repair my jaw that was set crookedly in Metz, and check my semicircular canals. I'm there at Fort Dix almost five months. When I'm not being examined and worked on, I finally get to use that typing MOS.

I'm put to work paying partial payments to all kinds of guys who are coming in, mostly from the South Pacific. They're being processed and discharged, processed like a word processor or a food processor. The army goes through their service records, calculates whatever money is owed them and debriefs them in a certain way, giving them the ruptured duck, we call it, an insignia indicating they are separated from the military with an honourable discharge. In the meantime, these guys, most of them with yellow skin from taking atabrine tablets, are waiting to be discharged. The atabrine was supposed to help them from getting malaria. Actually the pills didn't help, they only put off the symptoms.

The guys are given furloughs. For most of them it's been two, three or four years since they've been home. Usually they have no money. The army owes most of them a significant amount of salary, and it's piled up. But there's been no way they could actually get American money and spend it.

Generally there's no paymaster, that is if you were in an infantry outfit and in combat. What are these guys going to do? They can't even go buy a coke. It's really stupid and they're isolated at Dix without money.

So the military works out a system. The army gives them 'partial payments'. These are advance payments on what the military owes them. There's a Lieutenant Trout in charge of partial payments, but he's never there. He has a girlfriend and is gone all the time visiting with her. He puts me in charge. He should have known better than to do a thing like that.

I'm typing out partial payments of a hundred dollars each for anyone who wants them. They're going to give these guys three hundred dollars each, severance pay later, as well as back pay. They'd come up to me and give me their name, their service number and so forth so they can get the hundred dollars the army owes them. I'd type out what they tell me on a form, in triplicate. One I give them. This they're supposed to take to the paymaster for the money. One is supposed to be signed by Lieutenant Trout and put in our files. The third is to be put in their service records so it can be deducted from their money when they're discharged. I didn't! I'll never know how many partial payments I gave away, but I worked at that job while they worked on me for five months. I'd type the forms out, give them the one to get their money, sign the one that Lieutenant Trout was supposed to sign and 'round file' it, along with the one that's supposed to go in their service record.

For years, I expect the government to figure this scam out and come after me. After all, I've probably given away about fifteen thousand dollars. As far as they're concerned, it's completely disappeared. Compared to the way the military is spending money it's nothing, and who deserves it more? For about two years, I'm waiting for them to come, but they don't.

That one I can live with. This particular bit of villainy I might even still do today, given the chance or the nerve. As I say, at that time I didn't have much respect for virtually anyone. I was sort of an incipient psychopath, or at least, a misanthrope.

So this is the end of the tales I didn't tell, as I can remember them now, sixty years later. Some of them are humorous, many tragic, but in all of them I appear in a light I didn't want my children to see.

I'm not going to say I was the world's worst soldier. There were times when I performed reasonably well, considering what we were doing, killing people we didn't even know. When one is doing something as crazy and destructive as running a war, it's hard to behave well.

As long as you don't disgrace yourself too much and don't hurt anybody wilfully, it's more or less accepted in this life. But in a war, there's no way out.

Most of us, in one way or another, do both those things. One learns to live with it and do what one can to see it doesn't happen any more than necessary.

I never put notches in guns or anything like that. Some did. Other people had different kinds of wars than I did. I've met several guys who were in the infantry, in combat, and they say they never really saw anybody to shoot at. I can believe that. They probably gave cover fire, but never actually saw the enemy, or shot at him, on purpose, to kill him.

They were lucky. I can think of at least twenty times when that's exactly the situation I was in and there was no way out. As far as I know I've never had anyone shoot directly at me, look me in the eyes and shoot. If they did, I didn't know it, didn't get IT!

Bullets went sailing over my head or went someplace else. My trouble was shrapnel, I never really learned how to duck it, if that's possible.

I think in life, as I know it now, it's about the way it is. There aren't many people shooting to kill me or hurt me on purpose. They might kill me in an automobile, or by bad medical practice, but that's normal in our hectic lives.

However, the general shrapnel of the human condition has hurt me quite enough, more often and seriously than I'd prefer.

The shrapnel in most people's lives starts early, a rejection by a parent or loved one such as a good friend, not getting on the baseball team, not being chosen. The usual failures in the courtship rituals and trials, it goes on and on and sometimes if we're not careful we can become disabled, unhappy, distressed or depressed by the small wounds we suffer, often without anyone meaning to hurt us. So perhaps I should just call this book, **SHRAPNEL!**

I hope my kids enjoy these tales and won't lose too much respect for me. That would be like a land mine.

GLOSSARY

AGCT – Army General Classification Test
furlough – temporary unpaid
I&R – Intelligence leave and Reconnaissance
KP – kitchen police
MOS – Military Occupation Speciality
MPs – Military Police corps
non-com – non-commissioned officer
OD – olive drab, standard fighting uniform colour
PFCs – private first class
PX – post exchange
S2 – security
section 8 – discharge for being mentally unfit
SNAFU – situation normal: all fucked up
SP – Medical Specialist Corps